THE CHINESE PEOPLE
AND
THE CHINESE EARTH

The Chinese People
& the Chinese Earth

KEITH BUCHANAN
Professor of Geography, Victoria University of Wellington,
Wellington, New Zealand

LONDON: G. BELL AND SONS, LTD

ISBN 0 7135 0153 7

Reproduced and Printed in Great Britain by
Redwood Press Limited, Trowbridge & London

TO
My Mother
and to
the Memory of my Father

Contents

Maps and Diagrams

Plates

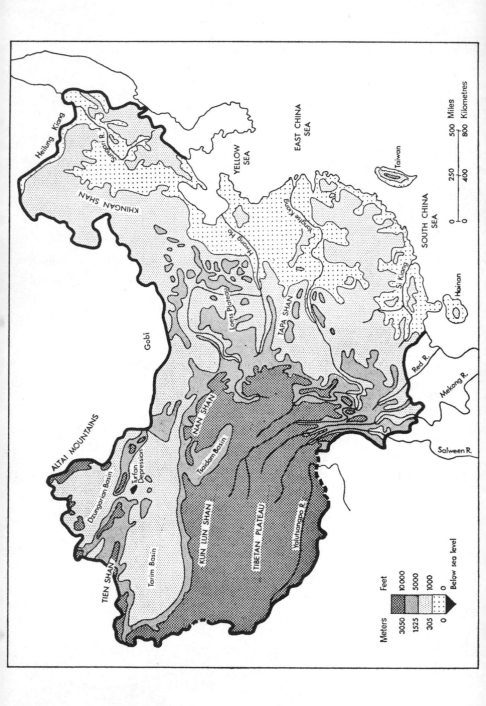

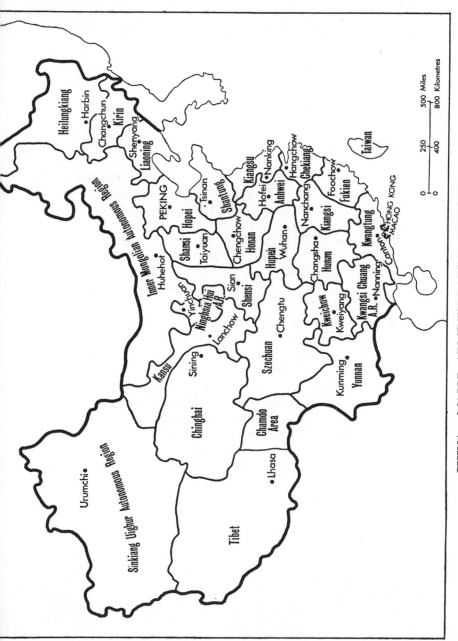

CHINA. MAJOR ADMINISTRATIVE REGIONS

Acknowledgements

THE WRITER has a multiple debt to acknowledge. First, to all those—commune chairmen and members, managers and workers in factories, members of Street Committees, scholars of the Academia Sinica and, above all, his interpreters—who helped him in his field work in China. Secondly, to those members of the Department of Geography in Victoria University who assisted in the preparation of the final draft of the work; to Mrs. Joan Elmes for patience and skill in typing and re-typing the drafts of the manuscript, to Mrs. Barbara Winchester whose cartographic skills are reflected in the maps, and to Mrs. Jean Benfield who was responsible for the exacting task of preparing half-tone illustrations from the author's Kodachromes, and, thirdly, to Miss Ann Stewart for valued assistance in the compilation of the Index. Finally, to Professor R. H. Kinvig whose courses gave the writer his first awareness of the true dimensions of geography and who gave him his first understanding of the Middle Kingdom.

All of these colleagues and friends have contributed to make possible this book; to all, the writer would express his gratitude.

KEITH BUCHANAN

CHAPTER 1

Introduction

TODAY, THERE are over 700 million Chinese; this means that one out of every four people in the world is Chinese. In terms of population alone China is the biggest nation on earth; whatever we may think of the Chinese government we cannot afford to ignore China. China is important in other ways too. Like the rest of the world outside the Western and Soviet blocs she is an 'underdeveloped' (or developing) nation, and by a 'forced march' which involves sacrifices for many of her people she is trying to build a modern nation—developing her industry, improving her agriculture, educating her children—in which people need never again be hungry or poor. She has chosen Communist methods to do this and many people in the West do not like these methods. In many of the under-developed countries, however, people are watching the Chinese experiment; if it is successful many of these countries may try to follow something like the 'Chinese road'. China is thus important as an example, as what planners call 'a develop-ment model', for the other underdeveloped countries. China is important, too, in the politics of Asia. As General de Gaulle has said of Asia, 'In this continent there can be no peace, nor any war imaginable without Chinese being involved'; since he spoke, China has developed nuclear weapons and is now the fifth nuclear power though, because of Western opposition, she is still excluded from the United Nations. And since we are all members of a world community whose future is increasingly shaped by the actions of each and every nation in this com-munity, we must know more about China. We must try to understand what the Chinese are trying to do and how success-ful they have been in their attempts to make China a modern and progressive nation. And perhaps we should stress that because we say we should try and *understand* this does not mean we say we should necessarily *approve*. The problems the Chinese have had to face are very different from the problems we face in the Western world; the way they have tried to solve *their* problems is, inevitably, very different from the way we try to solve *our* problems.

CHAPTER 2

The Chinese People

THE CHINESE people, or the Han people as they call themselves, have a very long history. Their civilisation developed almost 5,000 years ago in the middle reaches of the Yellow River. Its 'cradle area' was an area of fertile loess* soils, with 'islands' of harder rock protruding through this loess cover. It was an area which had many attractions to primitive man; its climate was equable, its soils good, the wooded areas of harder rock were a source of timber, water and building stone. To the west, the dryness of the steppe country was an obstacle to a farming people; to the south, in the Yangtse Valley and beyond, the dense subtropical and tropical forests were unattractive to the early Chinese (Map 1).

This Chinese culture was a composite one; it drew together elements from many other peoples and areas. Its chief food grains—wheat, barley and millet—it borrowed from the peoples of the Middle East; the use of bamboo, of iron, of the water buffalo and of terraced rice cultivation it learned from peoples dwelling far to the south, in the area the Chinese term the 'Nan-yang' (south seas); some of its religious practices were similar to those of the tribes who lived in the forests of what is today Siberia. These and many other elements were blended by the Chinese into a distinctive civilisation; this ability to take ideas from outside and give them a Chinese form is well illustrated today by the Chinese adoption of communism as the basis of their political and economic system and by its adaptation to Chinese conditions.

* The loess of North China is a yellowish grey loam soil with a high calcium content, derived by wind from the dust of the Gobi region. The loess soils are typically fertile with a good crumb structure and easy to work.

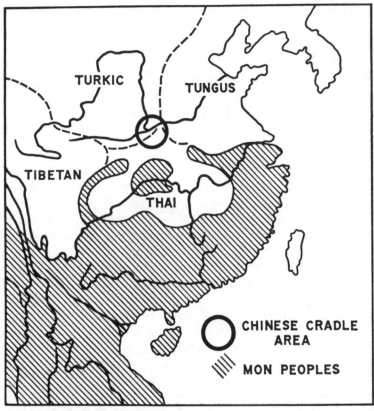

1. The Chinese Cradle Area *c.* 2,500 B.C. showing early centre of Chinese civilisation in the middle valley of the Yellow River. Most of South China at this time was occupied by Mon peoples, akin to some of the tribal peoples of south-east Asia today.

Gradually, as the generations passed, the number of these early Chinese increased greatly and the need for more and more land to farm forced large numbers to migrate. They migrated usually towards the south (for the west was too dry and the north too cold for their type of farming) and, as they did so, they came into contact with darker, wavy-haired, tribal peoples who occupied most of China south of the Yangtse River. The early Chinese migrants (seeking land and a living like the pioneers in the American prairies) were interested only in land on which they could continue their 'garden' type of farming. They occupied the river valleys and other lowland areas, pushing the tribal people either into the hills or to the south. It was a gradual process which went on century after century; the result is that today over much of South China the uplands are occupied by minority peoples, peoples whose appearance, whose languages and whose customs are very different from those of the Han people. The lowlands suited to intensive farming are, by contrast, closely settled by Han farmers.

To the north-west, the peoples of the grasslands were a constant source of worry to the Chinese. The Great Wall was built in an attempt to protect the settled lands to the south and east from the attacks of these nomads. Eventually, however, the Chinese were forced to bring all these people under their military control. They fought a long series of wars to establish this control and almost 2,000 years ago the frontiers of China

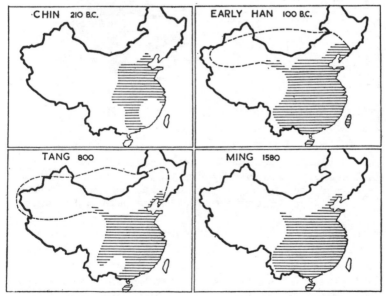

2. The Spread of Chinese Power at Various Periods. The hatched area indicates the area under solid Chinese political control; the dotted line indicates the area under looser Chinese suzerainty. The solid black line is the frontier of China today.

had reached their present extent. At this time the frontiers of the two biggest Empires in the world—those of Rome and China—touched in what is today Russian Central Asia.

China thus reached her present frontiers almost 2,000 years ago (Map 2). Moreover, as a result of her expansion she absorbed many peoples who were quite different from Han people, the people whom we usually think of when we use the

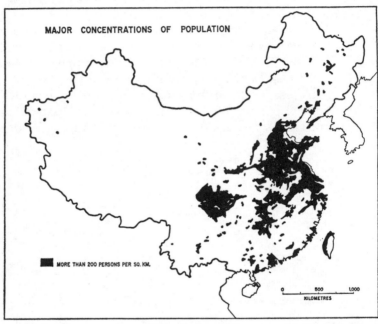

MAJOR CONCENTRATIONS OF POPULATION

MORE THAN 200 PERSONS PER SQ. KM.

0   500   1,000
KILOMETRES

3. Major Concentrations of Population. These are chiefly on the level lands of North China, the Red Basin and the Yangtse lowlands of Central China and the scattered plains and valleys of the south.

word 'Chinese'. These *minority peoples* include white-skinned peoples such as the Kazakhs and Uighurs (who later became Mohammedan) and dark-skinned slender people (rather similar to the Indonesians or to the Indochinese) such as the Yi or the Miao. These minority peoples total about 40 millions— but they occupy almost two-thirds of the area of China today (Map 6). China is thus a *multi-national state* and the old five-barred flag of the Chinese Republic symbolised this: the five bars represented the five most important groups—Chinese (Han), Manchu, Mongol, Mohammedan and Tibetan. In the past these minority peoples were often despised and oppressed; this is no longer so and the various minority groups participate with the Han people on a basis of absolute equality in the building of the new China.

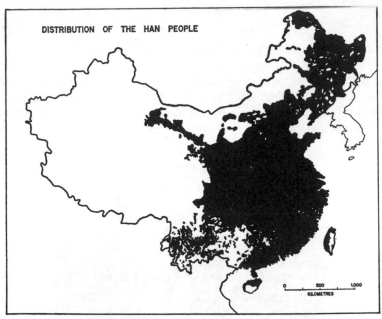

4. Distribution of the Han People. The Chinese, or Han people, are concentrated in the eastern, largely lowland two-fifths of China. In the north-west Chinese farmers have long been installed along the line of the Kansu Corridor; in the south-west, Han and minority peoples are complexly intermingled.

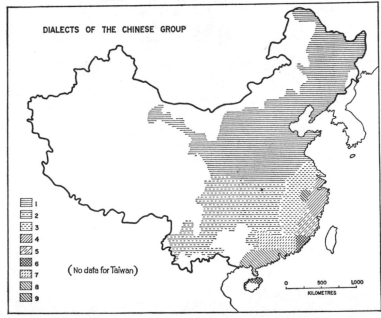

5. Dialects of the Chinese Group. Major contrast between the uniformity of the north (solidly Northern Mandarin in speech) and the complexity of the south.
   KEY: 1. Northern Mandarin. 2. South-western Mandarin. 3. Southern Mandarin. 4. Wu Group. 5. Foochow Group. 6. Amoy-Swatow Group. 7. Hakka. 8. Cantonese. 9. Anhwei Group.

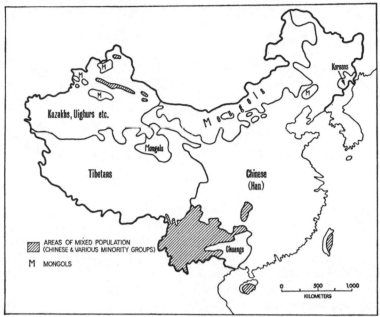

6. Major Ethnic Groups. Illustrating the major minority group, the Ural-Altaic of the west (Kazakhs and Uighurs), the Tibetans of the south-west, Mongols of the north, the Chuang of the south. In the south-west a great diversity of peoples.

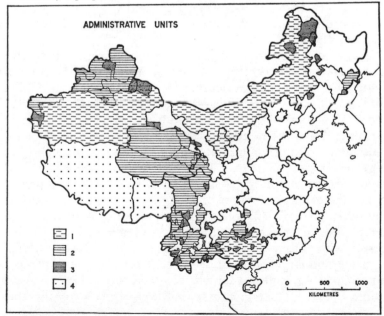

7. Administrative Units. Illustrating the progress of the various areas towards the highest level of autonomy—that of Autonomous Region. Comparison with Map 6 shows that some measure of regional autonomy has been granted to all the regions of minority peoples.

KEY: 1. Autonomous Region. 2. Autonomous *chou*. 3. Autonomous *hsien*, banner (*ch'i*) or area. 4. Region under preparation for regional autonomy.

CHAPTER 3

The Diversity of the Chinese Earth

W HEN WE think of China we tend to think of terraced rice fields or level, carefully-cropped fields of vegetables or millet or cotton. In fact, much of China consists of mountains, of deserts or of subarctic forest, and only a limited proportion is suited to intensive agriculture. China extends from 55°N to 17°N, the distance from Moscow to the south of Arabia; it extends from 500 feet below sea level in the depression of Turfan to over 29,000 feet in Mount Everest; its climates range from the perpetual frost climates of parts of Tibet to the rain-forest type of climate in Hainan Island and the extreme south. The Chinese people, in their expansion, were thus faced with a wide variety of environments, each offering particular challenges or opportunities.

The most important contrast within the Chinese living-space is the contrast between Inner China or Agricultural China and Outer China or non-agricultural China. In Outer China difficult physical conditions—lack of rain, poor soils, high mountains—make the area unsuitable to traditional Chinese farming; this is the domain of the pastoral nomad or the oasis cultivator. Outer China falls into two main subdivisions: the high-level tundra plateau of Tibet and the mountain ranges and desert basins of Central Asia and the Gobi. Over much of Tibet the general elevation exceeds 12,000 feet, the frost-free period is less than fifty days and in no month does the mean temperature exceed 50°F. Most of the area is a waste of frozen desert, with patchy shrub and grass vegetation. Its population is sparse, and largely nomadic with a life based on herds of goats and yaks. Agricultural land is confined to the lower valleys round Lhasa. The region may, however, contain considerable mineral wealth and its water power resources, concentrated where the Tsang-po breaks through the Himalayan chain, are among the greatest in Asia.

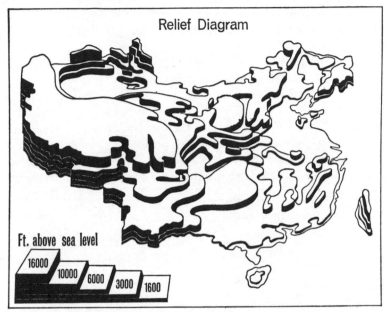

8. **Relief.** This diagram emphasises the contrast between Agricultural China and the Far West and within these two areas the contrasts between the Plains of North China and the hill country of the south and between the Tibetan Plateau and the basins and ranges to the north.

North of this Tibetan Plateau great mountain chains—the Altyn Tagh, the Tien Shan and the Altai—enclose the desert basins of the Tarim, the Tsaidam and Dzungaria. The chains rise to between 12,000 and 22,000 feet; the basins are below 600 feet, sinking in the Turfan Basin to 500 feet below sea-level. The lowlands all show a rather similar concentric arrangement of land types—a central plain of drift sand, an outer belt of better-watered scrub country and a discontinuous belt of oases nourished by glacier-fed streams. The steppe and desert country is the domain of the nomads, especially the Mongols, with sheep, horses and camels as the sources of wealth. New types of rationalised stock-rearing have been introduced, afforestation is providing sheltered conditions for farming, and improved and extended irrigation networks enable the farmer to take advantage of the five to eight months frost-free season. Agriculturally, this is a developing pioneer fringe area; it is, in addition, an area rich in metallic minerals and containing China's biggest oilfields.

Agricultural China is, broadly, China south and east of the Great Wall. Here rainfall is sufficient for cultivation and, though much of the area consists of rolling uplands or mountains, there are also wide lowlands and great alluvial and loess plains. Two themes dominate the geography of Agricultural China—the contrast between North and South and the contrast between upland and lowland. North China is tawny, dust-veiled and subhumid, with cold winters; it is the land of wheat

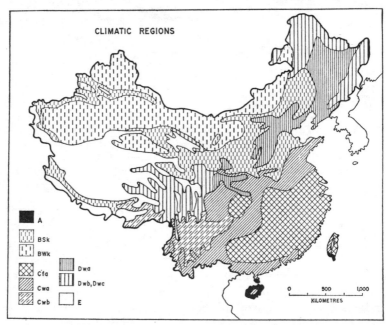

9. Climatic Regions. Emphasising the wide extent of semi-arid (B) climates and of tundra (E) climates. Much of Agricultural China falls into the mesothermal (C) group of climates, and the extreme south has a tropical (A) climate.

and millet, of cotton and soya beans. The South is green and humid, with mild or warm winters; it is the land of rice and tea, of bamboo and subtropical crops. Chinese cultivation is, we have seen, lowland or flatland cultivation and in both North and South the contrast between the hills and the plains is fundamental. For thousands of years men have concentrated in the lowlands and here every inch is cultivated; the hills, in contrast, repelled man and have been merely ravaged for their timber or left to minority peoples who practise a shifting agriculture.

From almost the beginning of Chinese history the most important area of 'flat-land' suited to intensive cultivation has been represented by the Loess Plateau and the Yellow River Lowland. The soils of these areas are formed from fine wind-blown or water-borne yellow-grey dust from the Gobi Desert. They are fertile, rich in lime and hold moisture well; this is important in an area such as this where rainfall is only moderate to low. Winters are cold and sunny and summers hot, with a frost-free period of between 150 and 250 days. These level loess soils have attracted farmers from very early times; so thorough has been man's transformation of the land by terracing and cultivation that no trace of the original vegetation remains. The only exceptions are the 'islands' of hard rock, such as the Shantung peninsula and the Taihang-shan, which protrude through the mantle of loess and alluvium and which carry a much cut-over scrub vegetation.

The tongue of mountains which extends from the Tibetan Plateau eastwards between the Hwang-ho and the Yangtse Kiang, the Tsinling-Tapa Shan, is one of the sharpest climatic divides in the world. In summer it is a barrier to the moisture-laden winds which move in from the south-east; South China thus has an adequate rainfall while the North is subhumid. In winter it protects South China from the icy winds which pour out of Inner Asia; in consequence, while winters in the North are bitterly cold, the South has mild subtropical winters. There are also topographic and soil differences between North and South. North China consists largely of plateaux or plains but much of South China consists of rolling hills. Level land suited for irrigated agriculture is confined to the floors of the river valleys or of old lake basins and, although man has extended his crop area by terracing, the area suited to intensive agriculture is only a fraction of the total; seen from the air, the landscape is one of long fingers of irrigated rice-lands probing deep into the scrub-covered hill country. The uplands, moreover, have soils which are generally poor and fragile.

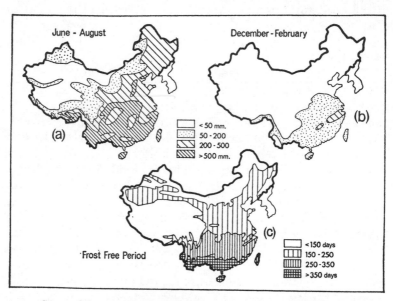

10. Some Climatic Features. General summer maximum of rain, Map (a), with heaviest falls in South China; some winter rain in South China, Map (b); virtually year-long growing season of extreme south contrasting with very short growing season of west and north, Map (c).

These soils are red or yellowish lateritic* soils and are much poorer than the loessial soils of the North; they are difficult to cultivate and their soluble plant foods have been removed by the heavy rainfall. The poverty of soils on the uplands, no less than their difficult topography, pushes man towards the valleys whose alluvial soils have been improved by centuries

* Laterites are red and yellow soils with a high iron content developed under conditions of heavy leaching in tropical and subtropical humid climates: they are characteristically acid, have a very low plant nutrient status and are difficult to work.

of manuring and cultivation and where the mildness of the climate makes possible two or even three crops of rice a year.

We have seen that for centuries the general direction of Chinese migration was southward from the Yellow River 'cradle area'. It was only in the closing stages of the last century that any significant northward movement began. This movement, directed towards the empty spaces of Manchuria, attained massive proportions in the first thirty years of this century; during this period some 30 million Chinese left their overcrowded homelands and moved towards this pioneer fringe in what was one of the biggest migrations in human history. The north-eastern sector of China is far from attractive climatically; its winters are harsh and long, so that in the higher areas the frost-free period is less than five months; the soils are for the most part poor and leached and great stretches are still under coniferous forest. But it is an area of great potentialities; the black and brown soils of the lowlands are excellent kaoliang (giant millet) or soya bean soils; its forests represent one of China's biggest reserves of timber; its deposits of coal, oil shale and iron were the basis on which the critically important South Manchurian heavy industry complex rested. This north-eastern region, with its reserves of unused arable land, may indeed play a role in China's development similar to that played by Siberia and the south-east steppe zone in the Soviet economy.

CHAPTER 4

Towards a Reappraisal of the Chinese Earth

THE RICHES of the Chinese earth are very great. They include resources of unused arable land; deserts and steppes that can be tamed; a diversity of climates making possible the production of almost every type of crop; a great range of rock formations containing almost every known metallic mineral; petroleum, oil shale, coal and unharnessed rivers to provide power; above all, the resource represented by the muscles and the minds of over 700 million people, a people whose civilisation is the oldest of the great civilisations of the modern world. Yet, in spite of this natural wealth, the average Chinese was abysmally poor and, though today he is emerging from this poverty, Chinese living levels are still so low as to make comparison with those of an 'affluent' nation such as Britain and the United States almost meaningless. For centuries, indeed, the Chinese peasant was like a beggar sitting above a vein of gold-bearing quartz, unaware of the wealth within his grasp, or incapable, because of poverty and lack of technical know-how, of converting the wealth into a form he could use.

China illustrates very clearly one of the most important concepts in geography, the concept that *natural resources are cultural appraisals*. Since 1949 the Chinese have trained many thousands of scientists in all fields—geologists, agronomists, geographers and the like—and their work is beginning to give us a much fuller picture of China's resource pattern than we formerly possessed. In particular, it is becoming clear that the old assumption of Western—and Chinese—experts that China lacked the broad range of minerals needed in a modern economy was quite erroneous; because we had little information about such resources we simply *assumed* China had little in the way of such resources. In the economic field, careful planning, resting on a clear-cut but flexible development policy, has for the first time mobilised the muscle power and mind power of China's hundreds of millions of people so that the country's precious human resources are no longer wasted through unemployment. Mass education and health campaigns are wiping out the wastage of human abilities which resulted from illiteracy or from illness. As a result of the changes since 1949 China's resources are being 'reappraised'—and a new geography of China, very different from the old geography, is beginning to take shape. We have space here for only a few examples of this process of reappraisal.

China's 'Wild West', the mountain and basin country of the west and the uplands of the south and south-west, is now known to possess a range of resources undreamed of twenty years ago. This vast area has been shown to possess major resources of natural gas and petroleum (perhaps rivalling the oil resources of the Middle East), of metallic and non-metallic minerals. These place China among the world's leading powers in terms of mineral resources and they represent the basis on which new industrial complexes are being built in this formerly neglected region of China. In this same western region scientific use of irrigation water (from the glacier-fed streams of the high mountains), afforestation and shelter-belt planting, and the use of aircraft in grassing the margins of the Gobi and other deserts are creating a new geography.

In Agricultural China science, by providing a better understanding of the best use of each environment and by developing new plant varieties, is changing the cropping pattern. Rice-growing, traditionally confined to the area south of the Hwai River, has been extended far north into Manchuria; winter wheat is now grown as far north as 47°N; the importance of the lower Yangtse valley as a cotton-producing area has declined and that of the Yellow River valley and of regions such as the Manass River valley in Sinkiang has correspondingly increased. In the extreme south, the expansion of the area under tropical tree crops such as rubber and cocoa underlines the new awareness of the agricultural potentialities of those limited areas of the country which have a truly tropical climate.

The development of these new resources, this 'reappraisal of the environment', affects not only the mining or agricultural sectors of the economy, it influences also the industrial geography. New mineral discoveries, new crops or the expanded output of crops already produced, the development of new sources of power, these make possible a much wider distribution of industry. The excessive—and strategically dangerous —concentration of industry in the eastern coastal districts is already a thing of the past and today each of the major economic regions into which China is divided (Map 17) has a considerable and expanding modern industrial sector. Economic diversification and the dispersal of industry have been key objectives of the present Government's economic policy; the work of geologists, geographers, plant breeders and the like has made it possible to begin to achieve these objectives.

1. Eternal China. Traditional Chinese architecture in the grounds of the Summer Palace, Peking. The hill on which these summer houses stand is an artificial one.

2. New China emerging, Kunming, Yunnan. The rice crop is being harvested; as soon as this is done the land is levelled for new housing development.

3. The Children of China. Han schoolchildren on their way to school in Peking.

4. The Children of China. Uighur school-girls from Sinkiang enjoying a break from school.

5. The Minorities of China. Miao girls from the south-western province of Yunnan in traditional dress.

6. The Minorities of China. Students and staff of the Institute for National Minorities in Lanchow. The students include Tibetans, Mongols and Uighurs.

7. South China. Green, humid and subtropical, with vegetable plots and clumps of bananas on the small areas of hill-girt lowland.

8. North China. Tawny, dusty and subhumid. Cotton field in the foreground, beans in the middle distance, bare and eroded hills in the far distance.

9.   The Hills of the North.   View from the Great Wall.   Open grassland country now being reafforested.

10. The Lowlands of the South.   Watering vegetables on a commune in Kwangsi.

11. The Pastoral Country of the West. Sheep-rearing on the grasslands of Chinghai.

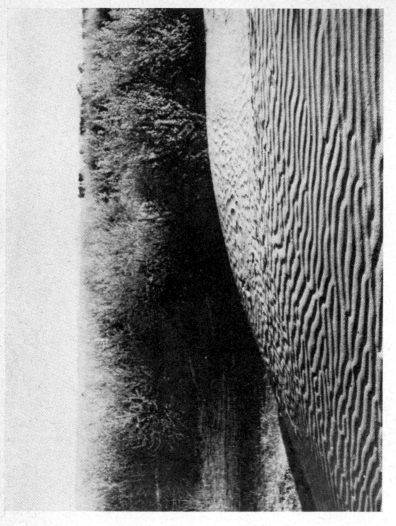

12. The Deserts of the Far West. Recently established shelter belts arrest the drifting sand.

13. The Red Basin of Szechwan. Old and New China juxtaposed, the factory chimneys and new housing rising behind the reed huts, the bamboo and the careful garden cultivation of Old China.

14. The Plateau of Yunnan. Wash-day beside a small stream on the high plateau of Yunnan.

15. Commune Headquarters in Kansu. Formerly a landlord's house, it is now the administrative and welfare centre of the commune.

16. Commune Headquarters in the Pearl River area. Again, the old and spacious house of a former landlord.

17. View across Commune close to Yellow River in Kansu. 'Oasis-style'
cultivation of vegetables and fruit, irrigated by ditches from Yellow River.
Old fortified village in the middle distance, with new buildings erected by
the commune outside the limits of the walls.

18. Uplands on the same Commune. These were bare and eroded and
are being brought back into productive use by anti-erosion measures (note
small dams across gulleys) and by the construction (by hand labour alone)
of scores of miles of terraces which are being planted with trees.

19. Part of Commune in Pearl River Lowland, South China. Intensive cultivation of vegetables with irrigation, in a climate where 8–10 crops of vegetables a year are possible. Members of a production team working in middle distance.

20. Part of Commune on North China Plain, near Peking. Careful preparation of hot-houses in which vegetables will be grown over the winter. The walls are of earth, the enclosures will be filled with manure and the plants protected by glass frames.

21. Man's Increasing Mastery of the Environment. Locks and dyke built by commune as part of the flood-control system in the Pearl River delta. This major project was carried through with peasant labour in the winter of 1960–1; it involved the shifting of 700,000 cubic metres of earth.

22. The Two Faces of Chinese Agriculture. On the top of the dyke the men are using the traditional technique of carrying—the pannier basket; the tractor and trailer at the foot of the dyke is one of the signs of mechanisation in the countryside.

23. A Traditional Industry: Silkworm-rearing on a commune in South China. The silkworms are entering the cocooning stage on the sloping trays of woven bamboo.

24. New Types of Industry. Construction of ovens for producing coke on a commune in the Kwangsi Chuang Autonomous Region. The new buildings in the background, including a school and a veterinary centre, were built by the commune, with the labour of its members and the funds saved from last year's operations.

25. Small peasant blast furnace on commune in Yunnan. Tens of thousands of these furnaces were built all over China in the intensive campaign to produce more iron and steel in 1958.

26. Forge on commune in South China. Workshops such as this not only cope with the maintenance of the tractors and other machinery on each commune, they also undertake the production of agricultural implements and various types of simple machinery needed by the commune.

27. Sulphuric Acid Plant on commune in Kwangsi. Built by peasants using local materials and with the technical advice of the chemistry master from the local technical school.

28. Rice-bowls for the Commune Members. This fifteen-year-old boy is making many of the rice-bowls used on the commune of which he is a member. He is here building up a bowl on a simple potter's wheel.

CHAPTER 5

The Changing Chinese Countryside

SOME FOUR-FIFTHS of China's population are peasants. In these conditions we cannot begin to understand China unless we know something of peasant life and its problems. These hundred million peasant families must not only produce sufficient food for themselves and for those of their countrymen who live in the towns; they must also produce, in addition to these food crops, raw materials for industry such as cotton, silk or oil seeds, a surplus for export so that China can buy the goods she needs for her industrial development, and a surplus sufficent to meet the demand of the State for taxes. It is these taxes, together with the profits of State-operated industries and State-trading organisations, which provide the Government with the funds needed to carry out the various aspects of its development plans. Agriculture is thus still the basis on which the whole economy rests; the progress of China in her 'forced march' to overcome backwardness and underdevelopment depends ultimately on the progress achieved in the agricultural sector.

We can get a graphic picture of the hopelessness and the corroding poverty of peasant life in Old China from the writing of many novelists; Pearl Buck's novel *The Good Earth* and Evan King's *The Children of the Black-haired People* are particularly valuable. For a more precise *statistical* picture, however, we must turn to the writings of agronomists such as J. L. Buck or René Dumont. The data given by the latter writer for a rural community in North Kiangsu illustrate admirably the character of the rural problem which faced the Chinese; his figures are summarised on page 34.

The total population supported by the community's 1,164 acres of arable land was 3,936; in other words, there was slightly

	Families	Arable land (acres)	Buffaloes
Landlords	12	1,089	—
Rich peasants	45	59	45
Middle peasants	11	16	26
Poor peasants and wage earners	845	—	3
Totals	913	1,164	74

less than one-third of an acre per person. 93 per cent of the land was in the hands of a dozen landlords and most of the villagers managed to live by renting tiny plots of land. Rents were very high—43 per cent of the value of a normal year's harvest, and even if the crops were ruined by flood the rent had still to be paid. The pressure of population was, as the figures above show, very great indeed; nevertheless a hundred acres of good farmland were not being used because the rents demanded were more than the peasants could afford. Because the peasant was

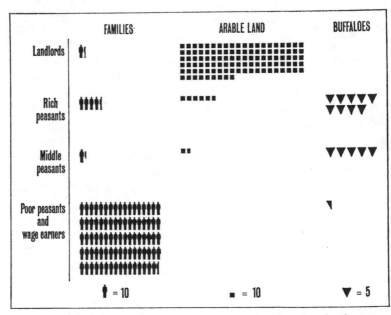

11. Cartogram illustrating distribution of land and work animals among the major classes in a rural community in North Kiangsu.

34

poor he could not afford fertiliser or adequate implements and so his crop yields were low—one-half of those achieved by rich peasants on similar land. The peasant was, indeed, caught in what Ritchie Calder terms the 'misery-go-round' of poverty—for poverty led to inefficient farming and inefficient farming led back to poverty. In good years, most of the peasants just managed to exist; in years of drought or flood they either stayed where they were and starved, or else joined the millions who roamed the Chinese earth in the search for food.

This one community presents in sharp focus the major problems the Chinese have had to tackle on the farming front: the uneven distribution of land; the exploitation of the peasants by the landlords; the human barriers, in the shape of poverty and high rents, which kept yields low and prevented man from making full use of the land; the helplessness of a backward and poverty-stricken peasant people in the face of natural disasters such as flood or drought. These various problems are closely interrelated; to take an obvious example, the problems of flood control and drought could not be solved by the individual peasant on his own for they called for cooperative effort and for resources which were quite out of his reach.

(i) THE RISE OF THE PEOPLE'S COMMUNES

The process of change in the countryside was begun by the land reform of 1949 which gave the land to the peasant who worked it; the landlord class, a largely parasitic group in contrast to the landlord class in, say, Britain, was thus abolished. But even though the peasants no longer had to pay excessive rents they still could not greatly increase output; some had land and no equipment to work it, some had work animals and not enough land to employ the animals fully, some still had plots too small to be worked efficiently. The development of cooperatives which pooled land, implements and work animals overcame some of these problems; the cooperative was a more efficient unit of land management and its development removed some of the social and economic barriers to expanding farm output. Even so, it was still too small a unit to tackle the really big problems facing the peasant such as flood control and the development of irrigation on a large scale. It was to tackle problems of this sort that the People's Communes were formed in 1958.

The commune was formed by the merging of numerous co-operatives into one large economic unit. The size of the communes varies; in 1958 the average population of a commune was about 20,000 people and the range in size from 10,000 to 100,000 people. The typical commune will contain perhaps scores of villages and sometimes small towns. It is managed by a committee elected by the peasants and it not only organises agricultural production, it also organises the welfare and educational services in its area, provides schools and technical

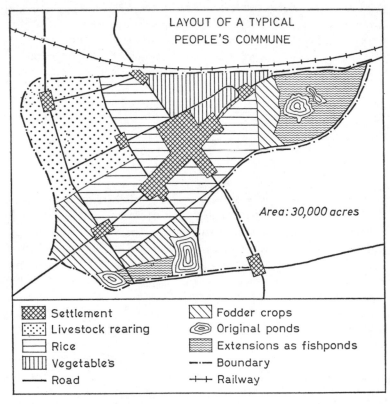

12. Layout of a typical people's commune illustrating the distribution of agricultural activities.

institutes, is responsible for the development of small-scale industry, for civil administration and for military defence. In 1958 there were 25,000 communes, formed by the merging of 700,000 cooperatives which had a membership of 110 million peasant families. Some of the communes in the hill areas proved too big to manage efficiently so these have been sub-divided in recent years; in consequence, the number of communes in 1964 is stated to be 74,000. There have been other changes, too, for Chinese planning has been flexible and quick

to learn from mistakes. Thus for crop production and budget-ing purposes the commune proved too cumbersome and for these purposes it is now broken up into *production teams* (con-sisting of some forty to fifty families in the South; some ten to fifteen of such teams form a *production brigade* and this now has the responsibility of implementing the policy of the commune in a given area and of organising education and welfare. Each commune consists of between fifteen and thirty such brigades and it is responsible for those activities which must be planned and carried out on a big scale: rural electrification, the mainten-ance of a pool of tractors, the management of rural industry. Another change has been the relaxation of the ban on individ-ual peasant production. Most of the land is worked by the

37

commune but today some 5 to 7 per cent is set aside as individual plots for the peasants' private use; most of the poultry-rearing and a good deal of the pig-rearing is carried on now by the individual peasant. In this field as in many others the Chinese are still experimenting; there is a good deal of variation between one commune and another and the system will continue to undergo continual modification and adjustment. Contrary to what many Western newspapers claim, these changes do not mean the commune system is collapsing; they are rather a sign that the system is very much alive and developing.

(ii) TURNING LABOUR INTO CAPITAL

The most important achievement resulting from this re-organisation of rural life was that it made possible *the mobilisation of China's labour resources*. China's 700 million people are perhaps her greatest resource—but this resource was only partly used in Old China which was one reason why the country remained poor and always perilously close to starvation. In the old days the peasant worked in the fields for from 50 to 250 days according to region; the rest of the time he was unemployed, either because there was no land for him to work or no industries to employ him. Yet even when he did not work he had to eat and it is obvious that, if a country has a large part of its labour force unemployed in this fashion much of the year, its chances of ever emerging from a poverty-stricken, hand-to-mouth existence are small indeed.

The development of the cooperative and the commune made rational use of this immense labour force possible for the first time. With the abolition of the old system of land-holding, farm work could be attended to by fewer workers, working full-time and with some specialisation; the labour of the remainder was made available, if only seasonally, for long-term improvements such as irrigation, terracing (Figure 18) or the creation of rural industries (Figures 23–28), all of which represented additions to the productive capacity of the countryside. In the words of a French expert, China's population became 'an enormous source of capital accumulation, devoting part of its labour to the increase of the productive potential of the countryside'. It is to this use of formerly wasted labour to create new industries, new irrigation systems, new afforestation areas and the like that the phrase 'turning labour into capital' is applied—for all these developments added to the *capital* of the rural areas, in that they were the means by which further wealth could be created. By 1958 unemployment had disappeared and electrification and mechanisation of farming were being pursued as a means of overcoming what was, in effect, a growing labour shortage.

This massive investment of labour is changing the face of China. It has made possible a large-scale attack on the problems of drought and flood which in the past made China a land of famine (the 1928 famine, caused by drought, resulted in 3 million deaths in the province of Shensi alone). In 1949, as a result of 3,000 years of development, China had 53 million acres of irrigated land; between 1949 and 1959 some form of irrigation had been introduced on 113 million acres; in the eighteen months ending with the winter of 1958 the Chinese brought more land under irrigation than in the whole of her earlier history. Water control and soil conservation projects have been undertaken on a massive scale all over China; the smaller projects are handled by the communes (who thus 'invest' the formerly under-utilised labour potential of the peasant masses in increasing the productive potential of the countryside), the bigger projects are undertaken by the State. The most striking of these projects is the Yellow River project which involves the building of a 'staircase' of dams which will not only regulate the river's flow but also generate large amounts of electricity (Map 13); this is linked with the rehabilitation of great areas of eroded land in the Yellow River catchment area. All these projects are examples of what the Chinese term the policy of 'walking on two legs', by which they mean the simultaneous use of traditional Chinese techniques and the most modern techniques, the integration of small-scale and large-scale projects, the collaboration of local bodies (such as the province or the commune) and the State in implementing development plans. It is by 'walking on two legs' that the Chinese have been able to achieve that steady economic advance which so many other underdeveloped countries are trying to achieve.

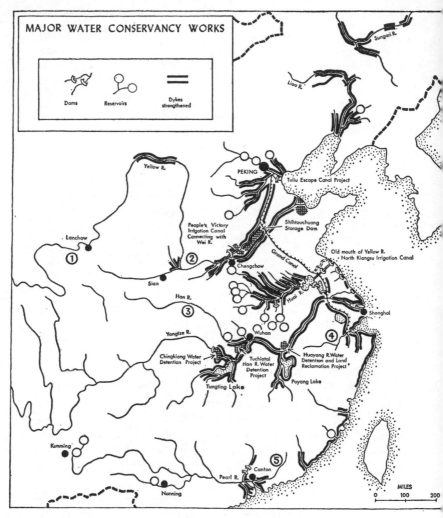

13. Major Water Conservancy Works illustrating the large-scale flood-control schemes and some of the more important hydro-electric projects completed or under way.

KEY: 1. Liuchia Gorge Project (in progress). Volume 4,900 million cu. metres. Power 1.05 million kw. 2. Sanmen Gorge Project (in progress). Volume 64,700 million cu. metres. Power 1.1 million kw. 3. Tanchiangkou Project (in progress). Volume 51,600 million cu. metres. Power 730,000 kw. 4. Hsinankiang Hydro-electric Station (in progress). Volume 17,800 million cu. metres. Power 652,500 kw. 5. Hsinfengkiang Hydro-electric Station. Volume 11,500 million cu. metres. Power 290,000 kw.

This same 'human investment' is transforming the vegetation pattern of China. Man has occupied much of China for thousands of years and by clearing for crops or cutting for fuel has destroyed much of the original vegetation. Less than one-tenth is today forested and, as living levels rise and more and more timber is needed, this limited area will certainly not provide sufficient timber for China's needs. Large-scale afforestation is therefore being undertaken and in this work literally millions of peasants have been employed during the slack period of the farming year. By 1957, 28 million acres were re-afforested; in 1958, 69 million acres (and a further 30,000 million trees planted around villages and along roads and river banks); by April 1959 another 39 million acres had been planted. In short, within 15 months, an area almost as big as France was afforested. The target for 1968 is to bring 500 million acres (one-fifth of the area of China) under forests. In the desert and semi-desert lands of China's Far West (and on the North China Plain too) shelter belt plantings have been made to protect existing cropland; sand dunes are being 'fixed' by new plantings (Figure 12) and wide areas of desert (four million acres by 1958) have been sown with grass from the air. 'Man,' say the Chinese, 'can not only conquer deserts but utilise them for his benefit' and this is what they are beginning to do in their Far West.

A third aspect of this mobilisation of labour on which Chinese development is based has been the war against disease, a war which has mobilised 100 million families in the attack on the parasites which crippled man or the pests which consumed his crops. Such an all-out attack on disease is of critical importance if the efficiency of farming is to be raised; in China, as in so many other underdeveloped countries, diseases such as malaria or hookworm immobilise the peasant at critical points of the agricultural year and are to a large degree responsible for the inefficiency of farming and the low yields. Here again, we come up against one of those 'vicious circles' in which many peasant peoples are caught: if you are frequently ill your farming suffers, if your farming is poor your crop yields are low and you'll not get enough to eat, if you are under-nourished you're more likely to fall a victim to disease. The Chinese are

41

tackling this problem by providing better water supplies in the country areas, by mass immunisation, by the training of medical and welfare staff and by a widespread educational and publicity drive. The campaign has been directed particularly against diseases such as malaria (mosquito-transmitted), schistosomiasis (the parasite for this disease has as an intermediate host a fresh-water snail) and hookworm (which enters the body through the feet); these were always major plagues in the subtropical south and have by now been largely eliminated. A similar campaign against pests such as flies, mosquitoes, rats and sparrows (the two latter major consumers of food grains) has achieved a remarkable success; indeed, in the case of sparrows it was *too* successful for if the sparrows eat grain they also eat caterpillars and elimination of the sparrows was followed by caterpillar plagues in many areas. But the general effect of this revolution in health has been similar to the effects of land reform or the control of flood or drought; it has lifted a burden from the shoulders of the country-dweller and, by eliminating a major cause of suffering and wasted human lives, it has added greatly to the productive potential of the Chinese peasant masses.

(iii) EXPANSION OF AGRICULTURAL OUTPUT

The commune system provided the framework within which improved agricultural techniques could be introduced. The basis of development has been in part the application of the measures set out in the so-called 'Eight-point Charter for Agriculture'.

Development has also been encouraged by the liberation of the peasant from old prejudices and attitudes through education; this liberation has expressed itself in a great number of peasant inventions such as improved tools, new planting techniques, and experiments in plant-breeding. All of these have helped to boost the output of agriculture. Another important factor has been the increasing control over the environment made possible by the extensive water control and irrigation schemes carried out in the last fifteen years; these have given a new stability to rural life.

Some of the technical developments, such as the use of improved varieties of seeds, increase food output without additional labour. Others, such as heavy manuring and close tending of each plant, involved the use of a much greater number of workers per unit area or crop land. This type of intensification, coming at a time when massive efforts were being made to industrialise the countryside, helps to explain the shortage of labour experienced in many parts of China in 1958. It then became clear that an increased degree of mechanisation was essential if progress was to be maintained. Such mechanisation takes many forms: many communes have tractor pools, and simple equipment, such as irrigation pumps and improved implements, is beginning to lighten the burden of pleasant toil. The Chinese objective is to mechanise all the land that can be ploughed or irrigated by 1969, though the achievement of this will depend to a large extent on the pace at which China's heavy industry develops. Chemical fertilisers are being used, though on nothing like the scale they are used in Japan. They are supplemented by 'natural' fertilisers such as pond mud, human excreta and massive quantities of commune-produced fertiliser (ranging from wood ash to crushed phosphatic rock); in this sector, too, agriculture is dependent on the expansion of

43

Deep ploughing

Adequate manuring

Irrigation projects

Good seed

Close-planting

Plant protection

Tools reform

Field management

The Eight-point Charter for Agriculture

heavy industry to supply the vast quantities of chemical fertilisers which are needed.

If we evaluate the results of the first decade of agricultural development under the Communist régime, it appears that much of the increase in production has been achieved by the intensification and improvement of traditional techniques within the framework provided, first, by the cooperative and, more recently, by the commune. This means that a very significant increase in production, both per unit-area and per capita, can be expected when the technical transformation of Chinese agriculture, involving heavy use of chemical fertilisers and widespread mechanisation, gets into its swing. Merely to cope with population increase, production must be increased by 2 to 3 per cent per annum; this can be done by either intensification, along the lines suggested above, within the existing agricultural area, or, alternatively, by expanding cultivation into the colder and drier margins of Agricultural China. The existing crop area is stated to be some 272 million acres and Chinese experts claim another 247 million acres is potentially cultivable though Western experts suggest a lower figure— about 100 million acres. Even if we accept this lower figure and bear in mind that much of this land may be less productive than land already cultivated, it is difficult to accept the common Western view that China is 'overpopulated' and faces an acute pressure of population on available land resources.

A broad picture of the evolution of agricultural production between 1949 and 1958 is given below (crops in millions of tons, livestock in million head):

	1949	1952	1954	1956	1958
Food crops	113·2	163·9	169·5	192·7	261·5
Cotton	0·4	1·3	1·1	1·4	2·1
Sugar Cane	2·6	7·1	8·6	8·7	—
Cattle	43·9	56·6	63·6	66·6	65·5
Sheep and Goats	10·3	61·9	81·3	92·1	112·5
Pigs	57·7	89·8	101·7	97·8	180·0

Source: Official Chinese statistics: Western estimates put the food crop output in 1958 at 220 million tons.

Accepting the scaled-down Western estimates for 1958 it is evident that food crop output almost doubled over the decade; on the basis of Chinese figures it increased almost two-and-a-half times. Livestock production showed an equally sharp increase. For the peasant, this increase in output meant a sharp rise in levels of living—in the form of a bicycle, a wristwatch or perhaps a sewing machine—and, above all, the beginning of 'community accumulation', in the shape of new implements, new housing, new school buildings. For the first time for centuries the peasant could feel that life had some purpose, that the future was his to shape. . . .

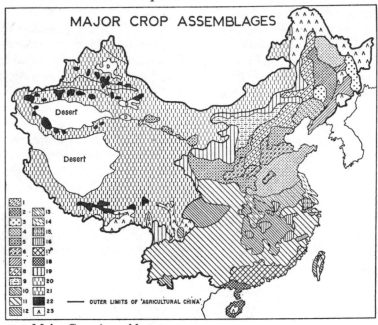

14. Major Crop Assemblages.
   KEY: 1. Cotton/Kaoliang; 2. Soybean/Kaoliang. 3. Kaoliang.
   4. Wheat/Oil Seeds. 5. Wheat/Miscellaneous grains. 6. Cotton/
   Wheat. 7. Maize. 8. Maize/Millet. 9. Potatoes/Grain.
   10. Rice/Wheat. 11. Rice/Maize/Timber. 12. Rice. 13.
   Cotton/Rice. 14. Cotton. 15. Rice/Wheat/Silk. 16. Tea.
   17. Rice/Sugar/Tropical fruits. 18. Rubber/Tropical Crops.
   19. Semi-farming/Livestock. 20. Desert Grazing. 21. Mountain grazing. 22. Oases of West (including agricultural area
   of Tibet). 23. Forest.

Between 1959 and 1962, however, China experienced an unprecedented series of natural calamities—floods, droughts and insect pests—and though no official crop statistics have been published there is no doubt that the expansion of food output ceased and that the output of food crops for these years dropped significantly. In the face of this situation the individual peasant would have been helpless; he would, as was the case when flood or drought hit Old China, have starved in his millions. The organisation of the commune system gave him the means to fight these problems by mobilising the rural population (and the Army) to fight drought and flood conditions, by digging new wells and by extending the dyke and water storage systems (Figure 21). Moreover, the Chinese government was able to buy—and to pay for—large quantities of overseas grain; it was also able to do what few Chinese governments could do and that is to see that the country's food supplies were fairly shared. It was a lean period—but there was no starvation and China emerged from it more than ever convinced of the advantages of the commune system. By 1963 crop output, from all reports, was once again moving upwards. By 1964 the grain harvest was described as 'one of the most satisfying in China's history', sugar production was two-and-a-half times that of 1963 and there was a glut of fruit and vegetables and a surplus of pork reported in some of the bigger cities.

(iv) INDUSTRY COMES TO THE VILLAGES

Much of the poverty of the countryside in Old China was due to the lack of economic diversification. Many of the traditional crafts were falling into disuse for they could not compete with factory industry and there were few jobs apart from those offered by a stagnating agricultural economy. An undiversified agricultural economy is rather similar to a single-storeyed house—it will accommodate only a limited number of people and soon gets overcrowded or overpopulated. The development of industry, of what is termed the secondary sector of the economy, is, to continue the simile, rather like adding a second storey to a house; many more people can be accommodated, can be fitted into the economy. And the development of services (teaching, medicine and other professions) increases still further the employment capacity of an economy, of an area; it's like adding a third storey to the house. Because they realised that undiversified economies mean poor people in a country as crowded as China, the Communist leaders have placed a heavy emphasis on rural industrialisation. This may take two forms —either the widespread decentralisation of large industry throughout the whole of China, or the widespread development of small-scale industries which are managed by the communes. The first form—decentralisation of large industries—we will examine later; here we are particularly concerned with the small-scale industries which became a major feature of the Chinese countryside after the development of the commune system.

These industries could draw on the great numbers of un-employed or under-employed in the rural areas for their labour; they could also utilise the tradition of craftsmanship which lingered on in the poorest village. Their development thus converted what had been a liability and a problem—the immense wastage of human energies created by a backward and highly seasonal agriculture—into an asset and a resource in the shape of tens of thousands of small enterprises employing millions of people in the production of goods desperately needed by the country dweller. They could use supplies of local raw materials which were too small to justify setting up

48

larger industrial units. They made it possible to economise on transport, for many of the needs of the rural dwellers for simple goods—household equipment or tools, for example—could be manufactured on the spot; this was critically important in a country where the transport system was strained to its maximum to meet the demands of the modern industrial sector.

The range of industries is very great and some indication of this is given by the details of sample communes in Appendix 2. It includes metal-working and the repair and maintenance of the commune's machinery (irrigation pumps, tractors, lorries, etc.), woodworking and bamboo work, manufacture of bricks and tiles, pottery-making, food-processing, and the manufacture of simple farm implements—in short, almost all the industries using agricultural raw materials or catering for the needs of a peasant population. The individual units are small but their aggregate importance is very great; by 1959, for example, these rural industries were accounting for one-tenth of China's total industrial output. They thus represented a very considerable addition to the wealth of the countryside and, what is even more important, they showed the peasant that industrial development does not necessarily depend on the specialist and the technician, on large-scale financial resources or state aid. With his mind and his muscle and the materials at hand the peasant could *himself* initiate the industrial revolution in the countryside; once this lesson has been learned, the psychological basis has been laid for an accelerating transformation of the face of rural China.

CHAPTER 6

China's Changing Industrial Geography

CHINA, ACCORDING to a recent American report, has a sufficiently diversified mineral base to become a first-rank industrial power. These resources are, moreover, widely dispersed over the country and, though we still do not know just exactly how mineral-rich many parts of China are (the geological mapping and stock-taking is still going on), we do know that many of the poorest areas in Old China have some of the most important mineral riches discovered to date. All this illustrates the point made earlier, that 'natural resources are cultural appraisals', that 'as the culture of the inhabitants changes, the meaning of the habitat changes'. In this context the 1949 Revolution in China marked the beginning of a new period in China's geography, for the new government initiated a systematic inventory of China's natural resources, an inventory still being carried on by geologists, soil surveyors, geographers and other scientists, an inventory absolutely essential if China were to become a modern, industrialised nation.

Large-scale industry in Old China has been aptly compared to 'a modern fringe stitched along the hem of an ancient garment'. As late as 1953 three-quarters of the country's industrial output came from the seven coastal provinces, and the cities of Peking, Shanghai and Tientsin. This coastal location of modern industry was due largely to the attraction of the Treaty Ports; parts of these were under foreign administration and so enjoyed a measure of security at a period when the rest of China was torn by civil war. In these parts, too, foreign industrialists found the advantages of an abnormally cheap labour supply and of access to supplies of raw materials and to markets. Except in Hankow and the north-east, the industries were chiefly light industries such as textiles, flour milling or tobacco manufacturing—but even in these products China's output was only a fraction of her needs. The output of means of production (such as textile machinery) was negligible; machinery replacements had to be imported and in these conditions China could never hope to stand on her own feet as an industrial power. Moreover—and this emphasised the dependent, semi-colonial, character of Chinese industry—much of the modern industry was foreign-owned (42 per cent of the cotton textile industry, 58 per cent of the shipbuilding, 63 per cent of the tobacco industry). This foreign domination extended also to the infra-structure—the communications and power system—for half of· China's railroad system was under the direct or indirect control of foreign capital, four-fifths of the coal production by modern methods and 57 per cent of the electricity, gas and water supplies.

Before the Second World War, then, the Chinese industrial economy was backward, geographically highly localised and partially dominated by foreign capital. The war against Japan, followed by the Civil War, reduced this flimsy structure to rubble; by 1949, according to one Western expert, the effective capacity of Chinese industry was zero. In the words of Mao Tse-tung, when the Communists came to power in 1949 Chinese society was 'a sheet of blank paper'; as such, it lent itself admirably 'to receiving the latest and most beautiful words and the latest and most beautiful pictures'.

(i) THE BASES OF INDUSTRIALISATION

The policy of rapid industrialisation rests on three bases: the natural resource endowment of China; the accumulation of funds, and the effective utilisation of the country's vast labour force.

As we have seen, China is still engaged in carrying out an inventory of her natural resources. Pre-Communist China had less than 200 active geologists; today, some 21,000 'geological workers', and some 400 geologists from other socialist countries, are beginning to give us a clearer picture of the country's mineral endowment. Their work has revealed mineral resources 'so extensive that they appear to make China one of the world's chief reservoirs of raw material'. Among the major discoveries is an unsuspected deposit of some 7,000 million tons of iron ore in Kiangsi (discovered by aerial prospecting) and a 3,000-million-tons deposit of high-grade ore (50 per cent iron oxide) in Honan. Coal resources appear to be inferior only to those of the U.S.S.R. and the U.S.A.; resources of non-ferrous metals, notably tin, tungsten and nickel, are among the largest

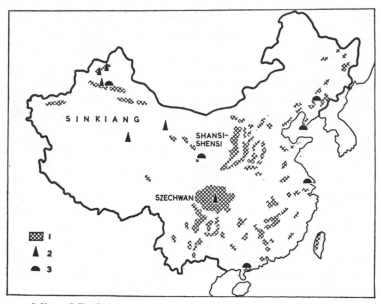

15. Mineral Fuels.
KEY: 1. Major Coal Deposits. 2. Major Oilfields. 3. Refineries

in the world. Petroleum production has expanded as the newly discovered fields in the Far West come into production and the country is approaching self-sufficiency in oil. The energy base is further strengthened by the hydro-electric potential of China's great rivers (110 billion kilowatt-hours on the Hwang-ho alone). To these resources we must add a wide range of other resources—synthetic and natural textile fibres, animal products, oil seeds and other food crops, all of which provide the raw materials for a diversified industry.

In the countries of Western Europe the exploitation of the

wage earner and of overseas territories (as, for example, through the slave trade) played an important role in the early process of industrialisation; it was partly through this exploitation that these countries were able to accumulate the initial wealth to invest in industry. In a country such as China, poverty-stricken, lacking overseas colonies, and with a socialist type of economy, the accumulation of funds needed to build a modern industry was bound to take a different form. Initially, a temporary source of investment funds was provided by the seizure of Japanese assets and the property of the landlord and *comprador* (middleman) group. However, the major source of development funds has been the profits of State industrial enterprises, of cooperatives and the State capitalist sector. Already, by 1955, taxes on the private enterprises which still existed provided only 11 per cent of the Budget receipts, taxes on agriculture 12 per cent and the remaining three-quarters came from the profits of the State-operated sector of the economy. Increasing productivity has made it possible not only to bring about a sharp increase in real wages (some 33 per cent during the First Five-Year Plan) but also to set aside increasing sums for development. The proportion of the national income set aside for this purpose, as opposed to the proportion made available for personal consumption, has been about one-fifth (or almost twice the figure for the United Kingdom). This austerity is, moreover, a shared austerity, participated in by all sectors of the community from the members of the Government to the members of the smallest commune. It is in large measure this austerity, this precise and abstemious budgeting, which has enabled the Chinese people to 'lift themselves by their own boot-straps', and to begin the process of industrial emergence with the very minimum of outside aid. It is this quality of self-reliance in economic development which most clearly distinguishes China from other emerging countries such as India.

The third resource on which development has been based is labour. We have seen how some of the achievements in the rural sector were the result of a process of 'turning labour into capital'. In the industrial sector likewise the rate of progress is partly explicable by the more effective use of existing labour resources and by the gradual but continuous rise in the level of technical competence. Between 1953 and 1957 non-agricultural employment rose from 36·5 million to 40·9 million. These overall figures, however, conceal considerable changes in the composition of this labour force; employment in handicraft industries declined, while employment in the modern sector rose from 15·6 million to 23·9 million and, within this modern sector, the number of workers in modern *industry* rose from 5·3 million to 7·9 million. The 'Great Leap Forward' in 1958 resulted in a huge growth in non-agricultural employment which rose in one year from 40·9 million to 58·3 million; the growth in the industrial sector alone was from 7·9 million to 23·4 million. *Thus, in one year, 15·5 million people moved into industry.* This terrific increase was largely due to the Chinese policy of using very large amounts of unskilled labour in place of scarce capital or skills to achieve the levels of production the planners had set; by the end of 1958 many industries had in fact reached the targets set for 1962. Since 1958 the emphasis of development has been not only on the expansion of production but also on the improvement of quality; to achieve this the Chinese are striving to raise the level of productivity of the labour force by a major programme of technical education. Such technical education is of critical importance in a developing country for, in a country such as China, where until recently virtually the entire labour force was illiterate and technically quite untrained, a rising level of technical competence may increase production as effectively as an increase in the labour force. The size of *this unexplored reservoir of technical efficiency* is as little known as the size of China's reservoir of mineral resources; that it may be very large indeed is suggested by the great number of improved techniques introduced by workers relatively new to industry and by the adventurous enthusiasm with which the Chinese are entering the new world of modern technology.

(ii) DESIGNING THE NEW INDUSTRIAL MAP

The first task which confronted the People's Government when it came to power in 1949 was to rebuild the shattered economy of the country. The initial target was to regain the

1943 level of industrial production by 1952; this target was in fact exceeded and industrial production in 1952 was almost one-quarter higher than in 1943. From this point the development of the country proceeded by a series of Five-Year Plans which aimed at transforming China from a backward agrarian country into an advanced socialist industrial nation, if possible within the space of three such quinquennial plans.

To create an industrial economy from the ruins of a peasant economy implied a heavy emphasis on industry as opposed to agriculture. Since agricultural production itself had to be expanded to provide a rising level of rural living and some of the funds and raw materials needed for industrialisation, it followed that a very rapid rate of growth in the industrial sector was essential from the beginning. Moreover, since China was determined to create a balanced and self-sufficient industrial economy, a strong emphasis on heavy industry, and especially the machine-building industry (whose development would enable China herself to produce the equipment needed in other industries), was essential. Almost nine-tenths of the investment in industry went to the producers goods industry, and slightly over one-tenth to the consumer goods industries (textiles, shoes, etc.); such an allocation of resources illustrates a point made earlier—the determination of the Chinese not to allow the natural desire for rapidly rising living levels to divert funds and energy from the more critical task of building firmly the economic basis for a self-reliant and expanding economy. Between 1949 and 1959 the aggregate output of agriculture and industry increased fivefold; between the same dates the gross output value of industry increased twelvefold. By 1959 industry accounted for two-thirds of the gross output value of agriculture and industry, as compared with less than one-third in 1949; moreover, as early as 1957 over half the industrial output consisted of producers' goods, of machines to manufacture all types of industrial products. The Chinese are thus in the process of achieving two of their objectives—industrialisation and economic independence. They have also made major progress towards achieving their third aim—the correction of the lack of balance in the geographical distribution of industry by developing the interior districts.

The old pattern of concentration in the coastal areas bore little relationship to either the resources or the needs of China; it was a pattern resulting from two factors: first, the political stability of the Treaty Ports, secondly, the very high profits which industrialists could obtain by exploiting the impoverished and abundant labour force piled up in these cities. The pattern of industry since 1949 has, in contrast, been a planned pattern, one whose character has been determined by certain

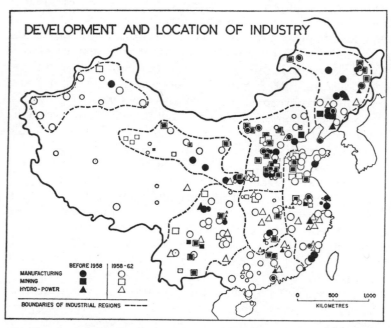

16. Development and Location of Industry illustrating initial concentration in east and north-east and diffusion of industry southwards and westwards after 1958.

principles of industrial location followed by planners in most socialist countries. These principles are: the siting of new projects near raw material and fuel sources and, if possible, consuming centres in order to cut down transport; the widest possible distribution of industry, thus reducing the differences between the industrial and rural sectors of the population and, more especially, between minority and majority groups; the need to achieve a better balance between industry and agriculture in each major economic region; finally, the strategic need to avoid the exposed and vulnerable coastal regions. The application of these principles has resulted in an industrial map quite different from that of China in 1949.

The policy of industrial dispersion towards the interior took shape with the First Five-Year Plan (1953–7). Existing centres such as Shanghai and the North-eastern Region were strengthened and modernised; their industries played an important role as sources of funds for the construction of new industrial centres in the interior. The main drive of industrialisation, however, was towards the west and north-west (Map 16). Two-thirds of the major industrial enterprises during the First Five-Year

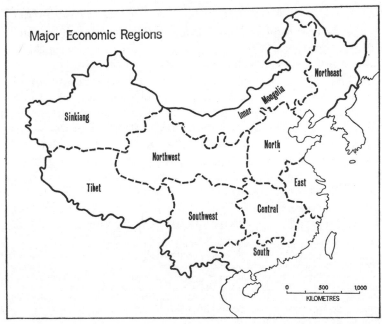

17. Major Economic Regions. These are the basic regions in the economic planning of the country. The Chinese aim is to build up a diversified and balanced economy within each such region; this implies a balance of industry and agriculture, of light industry and heavy industry and the development within each region of the energy bases on which industry must rest.

57

Plan were constructed in the interior; here, between 1953 and 1955, output increased 96 per cent as compared with 55 per cent in the coastal areas. The most striking manifestations of this drive have been the creation of a new iron and steel complex at Paotow in the grasslands of Inner Mongolia; the development of a major industrial complex centring on Lanchow (Figure 31) in the north-west and the intensified development of the oil resources of the Far West and the coalfields of the north. A similar process of industrial advance is following the uncovering of new resources in the uplands of South China; here the resources include coal, oil and non-ferrous metals and the first stage of this development is represented by the rise of a new industrial region in Kwangtung.

(iii) THE PACE & CHARACTER OF DEVELOPMENT

The pace of industrial development has few parallels among the other nations of the world, 'developed' or 'developing;' it is, for example, significantly greater than that achieved by the U.S.S.R. at the comparable stage of *her* development.* Between 1949 and 1959 the gross output value of industry increased twelve times and by the latter date industry was contributing an estimated two-thirds of the country's gross output, agriculture one-third. The First Five-Year Plan set as its target in industry an increase in production of 98 per cent over the 1953 level; this meant a yearly growth rate in the industrial sector of almost 15 per cent and the achievement of an industrial output of some 54 billion *yuan* by 1957. The figure in fact achieved in 1957 was an output of 65 billion *yuan*. The

* The development of Japan since the middle of the nineteenth century could also be cited as another example of a 'forced march' to industrialisation. As in the case of China, the success of development was due partly to strong centralised planning (within a social framework which brought together, incongruously, capitalistic and feudal ideas); like the Chinese, the Japanese depended for the accumulation of development funds on the rural sector. But the size of the population concerned was much smaller (in 1860 the Japanese population was only one-twentieth that of China in 1960), the Japanese did not have to face the problems left by twenty years of war and civil war, nor the virtual economic blockade by a large part of the industrialised world. Even given Japan's relatively favoured situation "growth for a long time [was] slow, but periods of marked impetus coincided with opportunities presented by the World War of 1914-18 and the preparations for the Second" (H. J. Wood in *The Changing Map of Asia*, ed. W. G. East and O. H. K. Spate, London, 1953, p. 295). A comparison of the processes of modernisation in China and Japan will be found in S. Kuznets *et al.*, *Economic Growth: Brazil, India, Japan* (Durham, N.C., 1955, Chapter 17).

Second Five-Year Plan (1958–62) aimed at doubling industrial output over this period; the planned increase in agricultural production over this period was to be 35 per cent so there was to be a continuing heavy emphasis on industry. The 'Great Leap Forward' in 1958 resulted in a sharp increase in this already rapid rate of expansion; in consequence, many of the targets set for 1962 were actually achieved by the end of 1958. The absolute levels of production achieved in some of the major industries over the period 1952-58 are summarised below

Production in Selected Industrial Sectors, 1952–58

	Unit	1952	1954	1956	1958
Electricity	Bill. kWh.	7·2	11·0	16·6	27·5
Coal	Mill. tons	63·5	79·9	105·9	270·0
Pig Iron	Mill. tons	1·9	3·0	4·8	13·7§
Steel	Mill. tons	1·3	2·2	4·5	8·0
Machine tools	Thousands	13·7	15·9	26·0	50·0
Cotton Textiles	Bill. metres	3·3	4·5	4·6	5·7

§ Of this, 4·16 million tons was low-grade pig iron produced by peasant methods.

A clearer picture of the relative pace of development in various sectors is obtained if we convert the figures to indices with 1952 as base year: 100. For 1958 the index for coal was 425 (i.e. production increased four and quarter times during the period), for electricity 380, for steel 593 and for machine tools 364. Production of consumer goods expanded more slowly; to take two examples, the index for cotton textiles was 174, for cigarettes 179. This is partly a result of the deliberate priority given to producer goods; in the case of textiles the disappointing cotton harvests may also have contributed to this slowness of growth. By 1960 China was producing virtually the entire range of modern industrial products, from antibiotics to heavy electrical generating equipment, from quality knitwear and ceramics to tractors, aircraft and medium-tonnage merchant ships (Figures 29–32).

The very pace of this development and this broadening front of advance, in a country still short of technicians and specialists of all sorts, present many problems, not the least being the uneven quality of production in some industries and the inefficient use of plant. Difficulties of this nature, coupled with the sudden withdrawal of Russian aid in 1960 and the impact of three years of reduced harvests on the light industry sector, led between 1960 and 1963 to a slackening of the pace of industrial growth. The Chinese have learned that ultimately an emerging nation must build on a basis of self-reliance, that its industry is ultimately limited by what its agriculture can produce, that, as Chen-Yi has put it, 'agriculture and industry must go forward together so that each helps the other'. All this has meant that those branches of industry which did not give quick returns were cut back or halted, while priority was given to branches 'whose immediate help to agriculture or immediate returns from the consumer would increase the rhythm by which gains in agriculture fed industrial gains'.

Before 1949 China made few machines; at the most she assembled imported parts. Today she is able to supply all the machinery and equipment needed in twenty major industries. She manufactures trucks and buses, jeeps and small cars, ships, trains and aircraft. She is 95 per cent self-sufficient in rolled steel, 90 per cent self-sufficient in machinery and practically self-sufficient in petroleum. Her chemical industry, producing fertilisers, plastics, synethetic fibres and semi-synthetic antibiotics, is one of the booming industries. Traditional Chinese textiles, such as silks and brocades, are finding expanding markets overseas; at home, synthetic fibres and wool supplement cotton and every province except Tibet has its own textile industry.

The Chinese economy is still not yet a giant economy, proportionate to the needs of 700 million people. But it is modern, self-reliant, and includes nearly all branches of production. It has emerged from the difficulties of the last five years strengthened and streamlined, and is in the process of take-off into a future whose shape will be determined by the discussions that are going on in every factory, every commune, every gathering through the length and breadth of China. Take-off to where? To a society dominated by the quest for affluence and the craving for more and yet more gadgets? To a world society in which man can rise to his full stature as a human being, recognising that this is impossible as long as half of his fellow men, the peoples of the 'underdeveloped' nations, still live travesties of a human life? These are some of the things occupying the Chinese and which, in part at least, account for the ideological rift in the Sino-Soviet bloc.

(iv) 'WALKING ON TWO LEGS'

One of the distinctive features of China's industrial revolution has been the many-fronted advance of industry. Existing plants are being extended; new large- and medium-scale factories are being established; and alongside this modern, large-scale, industrial sector the productive capacity of peasant or 'native-style' industry is being used to the full. This policy of 'walking on two legs' (p. 39) is one of the biggest contributions made by the Chinese to solving the problems posed by poverty and economic backwardness; it is a policy which gives the geography of New China a personality quite different from that of most other underdeveloped countries who have been content to follow Western models of economic development (which involves capital-intensive and geographically highly concentrated industry, in contrast to the labour-intensive and dispersed industries of Chinese planning).

This policy of 'walking on two legs' is illustrated very clearly by the development of hydro-electricity. China is building, or has completed, some of the biggest and most modern hydro-electric generating stations in the world—the Sanmen Gorge and Liuchia Gorge projects on the Yellow River (combined capacity over 2 million kilowatts) and the Tanchiangkou project on the Han River in Hupeh (Map 13). Alongside these, commune members have built a great number of very small generating stations; these accounted for one-half of the 2 million kilowatts added to the country's installed capacity in 1958. The advantages of these small projects are numerous: they spread the centres of power supply evenly over the countryside, they speed up the technological revolution in the countryside, and by providing power they ease the labour situation. They require only a small head of water, can be built with local materials and local labour and in their construction and operation the peasant acquires experience which will be of major value when larger and more complex hydro plants are built. Similarly in the steel industry advance has been achieved, on the one hand, by the creation of large-scale integrated iron and steel complexes of the most modern kind; on the other, by the massive experimental development of medium-scale and small-scale 'native-style' blast furnaces (Figure 25), which could draw on seasonally available labour and use resources of fuel or ore too small to justify the establishment of a major industry.

This policy has enabled the State to concentrate its limited resources of capital and technical skills on the development of large-scale modern industry. It is a policy which has social advantages also. It is easy to see that, in a country the size of China, the creation of a series of giant industrial complexes would have only a limited social and technological effect, for the majority of the rural population would remain cut off from the industrialisation and mechanisation which are the bases of modern life. The policy of dispersal, of 'Walking on two legs', avoids the creation of a new 'technocracy' in the heart of the countryside and makes possible the maximum diffusion of new techniques and new ideas among the peasant masses. It thus lays a firm foundation on which an accelerating 'technical transformation' of rural China can be based.

CHAPTER 7

The Consolidation of the Transport Network

L ACK OF an adequate transport system was a major obstacle to development in Old China. There was little in
the way of an integrated network, merely a system of un-
connected links by road, rail or water. The greater part of the
mileage was concentrated in eastern China and great sections of
the interior were without modern transport of any kind; the
north-west and south-west together had fewer than 500 miles of
railroads. Such conditions made the development of a national
economy impossible; the country remained broken up into a
series of more or less developed areas, separated from one
another by a stagnant sea of subsistence production; the
resources of the interior were inaccessible; the creation of any
real unity between the various peoples of China was impossible
because of the complete isolation of many groups.

In these conditions it was inevitable that the Communist
government should devote considerable funds to the creation
of an integrated transport network. A total of some £1,200
million, or one-fifth of the expenditure on the First Five-Year
Plan, was accordingly allocated for the consolidation and
modernisation of the transport network. By the end of the
1950s the broad lines of China's new transport system had been
laid down.

The end of the Civil War in 1949 marked the end of almost
twenty years of war and civil war. During these two decades
the railway system had been reduced to chaos. Between 1949
and 1952 the new Government directed its efforts to rehabilita-
ting the old system; from 1952 onwards it pushed ahead with

improvements in the shape of the double-tracking and the re-laying of many of the lines and with the building of new lines to open up hitherto inaccessible regions and to link together disconnected segments of the old system. The major lines are the Lanchow–Sinkiang (Lan-Sin) line which will run westwards through Sinkiang to link up with the Soviet rail system and which links the north-western oilfields with the main centre of population in the east of China; the Lanchow–Paotow line which links up with the rail system of the Mongolian People's Republic and gives access to the Paotow iron and steel complex and the mineral and agricultural resources of Inner Mongolia; the Chining–Erhlien line which links North China with Outer Mongolia and the U.S.S.R.; and the Paochi-Chengtu line which provides a much needed North–South link across the

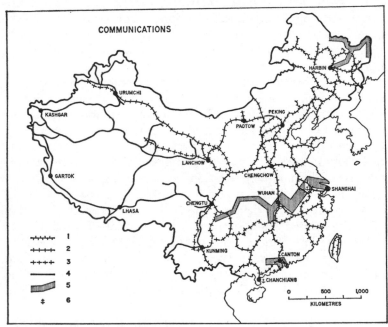

18. Communications (excluding airways).

KEY: 1. Rail network before First Five-Year Plan. 2. New lines completed since 1952. 3. Lines projected and in construction. 4. Major road links in Far West. 5. Navigable waterways. 6. New Ports.

29. The Rise of Chinese Heavy Industry. Part of the exhibition of Chinese-made machinery in Peking, 1958.

30. Light Industry. Part of the Peking Woollen Mill.

31. An Expanding Energy Base. Oil tanks at the new oil-refineries at Lanchow, Kansu Province.

32. China becomes a ship-building nation. The first 10,000-ton ocean-going freighter built by the Dairen (Talien) shipyard.

33. Children of a kindergarten run by a Peking factory.

34. Mothers with children in a factory crèche. The girl on the right is a Hui girl, belonging to one of China's national minorities and being trained in this textile mill before returning to her home district.

35. Contrasting Types of Rural Settlement. Small hamlet north of Peking; stone-built with tile roof.

36. Contrasting Types of Rural Settlement. Village street in Yunnan; mud-brick houses with curved tile roofs.

37. Old Peking. The Forbidden City, containing the former Imperial Palace and now a national museum.

38. New Peking. Multi-storied flats and offices replacing the old single-storey housing.

39. Old Peking. One side of a Peking street, with traditional style housing.

40. New Peking. The other side of the street: new multi-storey offices, built in a style which suggests Soviet influences. This sort of dramatic contrast within one street is indicative of the great changes transforming the Chinese capital.

41. Old Lanchow.   Back street in this old oasis city which grew up on the Silk Road to the West.   Low mud-brick architecture with thatched or tiled roof.

42. New Lanchow. New office blocks in process of construction a few streets away from Figure 41. Roads and major services such as water being put in; massive use of human labour.

43. Old Nanning. Part of the old city close to the river.

44. New Nanning. Modern hotel completed in late 1950s as part of the rebuilding of the city centre. Contrast this more florid architecture with the austere architecture of parts of New Peking.

45. Old Kunming. Wooden houses, cobbled streets—and recently planted trees.

46. New Kunming. Five minutes' walk from the area shown in Figure 45. Multi-storied offices and flats, colour-washed and gay; concrete dual carriage-way with flower-beds down the centre. Early morning with children on the way to school.

47. Old Canton.

48. New Canton. Workers flats in the city suburbs (1958).

49. Tibetan actress (woodcut by Li Huanmin).

50. Girl of Tung nationality (woodcut by Ho Yun-lan).

China's peoples as seen by Chinese artists

51. Terraced landscape in
South China (collective
work).

China's landscapes through the eyes of her artists

52. Kweilin Landscape (Hu Jo-ssu): steep lime-stone crags rising above terraced rice-fields.

China's landscapes through the eyes of her artists

53. Winter in the Taihang Mountains (Lu Tsun-pei): underlining the severity of the winter in the uplands of North China.

China's landscapes through the eyes of her artists

54. Gathering Mulberry Leaves (Wu Chun-chi).

55. Gathering Water-chestnuts (Huang Chou).

56. Tea-pickers (Hua To).

Scenes of daily life illustrating the diversity and subtropical character of the South Chinese landscape

57. 'The Peacock Princess': The Chinese film industry, including the cartoon film, is bringing the
legends and the music of the minority peoples into the
main stream of Chinese mass-culture. This is a scene
based on one of the folk-tales of the Thai tribes of south-
west China.

uplands of Western China. Smaller lines, especially in the south, have opened up the agricultural and mineral resources of the interior and given the South outlets at Amoy, Swatow and the new port of Chanchiang. Some 1,500 miles of new railroad were added to the system in 1958 and over 6,000 miles during the Second Five-Year Plan.

Some 46,000 miles of negotiable trunk roads existed in 1949. Between that date and 1962 almost 90,000 miles of new roads have been constructed, three-fifths of the total being in the minority regions of the West. Some of the new roads, such as the Chinghai-Tibet and Sinkiang-Tibet roads, are major engineering feats, crossing difficult terrain over 14,000 feet above sea-level. Here, and in Yunnan, the development of the road system makes accessible new resources; it also contributes to the effective unification of the State territory. Full utilisation of this expanded road system hinges obviously on an adequate lorry fleet and here the expansion of China's vehicle production (with major centres at Changchun and Peking) is critically important. And, in the transition period to a fully mechanised transport system, traditional forms of transport—5 million mule carts or horse carts and 10 million hand carts—play a vital if humble role.

The great rivers of China—the Si Kiang, the Yangtse Kiang, the Heilungkiang and the Sungari—offer important lines of communication in an East–West direction. Together with the complex network of smaller rivers they give China some 60,000 miles of navigable waterway. During the First Five-Year Plan 25,000 miles were opened to navigation by steamer, the navigable channels of the Pearl River, the Yangtse Kiang and the Heilungkiang were dredged, and new harbours opened at Chanchiang in Kwangtung and Yushikou on the Yangtse. During the period of the Second Five-Year Plan the reconstruction of the Grand Canal was undertaken so as to provide a major North–South waterway which complements the river system. When completed it will link five rivers—the Hai Ho, the Hwang Ho, the Huai River, the Yangtse Kiang and the Chientang—forming an integrated water transport system covering almost half of China; Peking will become an important inland port, connected by water with cities as far south as

Chengtu. The various large-scale water conservancy schemes contribute also to the expansion of the network of internal waterways (Figure 21); to take a single example, in North Anhwei a carefully planned system of drainage canals is providing also almost 80,000 miles of waterways navigable to small steamers and junks, linking together all the townships and communes in the area.

Given the size of China, its difficult terrain, and the still skeletal character of the road and rail system in the Far West, air transport is of vital importance. A relatively dense network of air routes has been developed as illustrated in Map 19 with

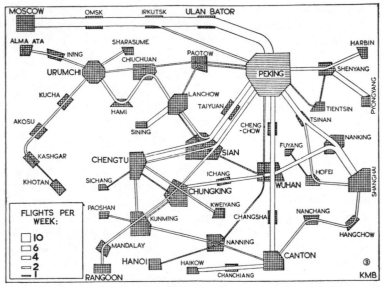

19. Cartogram showing the Chinese Airways *c.* 1960. Thickness of line is proportionate to number of passenger flights per week.

Peking, Wuhan and Sian as the main 'nodes' and with secondary nodes at Urumchi, Chungking and Lanchow. External air routes link China with Hanoi, Rangoon, Khotan, Alma Ata and Moscow; in the last few months new links have been established with Paris, Phnom Penh, Karachi and Tokyo. Within China, the plane, more than any other factor, has integrated the sparsely settled Far West with the remainder of

China; distances from Peking to the cities of Outer China—
Kashgar, Aksu or Hami—are now measured in hours rather
than the weeks which were involved when travel was by land.
This greatly increased speed of communication with outlying
regions is of major importance in a country developing at
China's pace; technicians, blue-prints, delicate precision
equipment can be rushed by plane to development areas where
other transport might take weeks. Civil aviation is helping
too, in a wide variety of other fields—surveying, geophysical
prospecting, pest control, afforestation and the sowing of grass
seed. The plane, in short, has become a vital instrument in the
transformation of the Chinese earth; its development is one
example of those processes of cultural and technological
change which are making possible a complete reappraisal of
China's resource endowment.

CHAPTER 8

Population: Problem or Resource?

CHINA WENT through a political revolution fifteen years ago; she is now going through a second revolution—a demographic revolution. This demographic revolution is bringing about vast changes in the population of the country and is in part a consequence of the political revolution. Daily life is more certain and more secure; disease is being brought under control by the application of modern medical techniques so that old folk are living longer and more children are living through the critical years of early childhood. Death rates in Shanghai, for example, dropped from 19·4 per thousand to 6·7 per thousand between 1953 and 1959.

Now, the rate of population growth in a country depends obviously on the balance between the death-rate and the birth-rate. If the death-rate falls, and birth-rate remains high, the population will grow in numbers; if the birth-rate drops below the death-rate the population will gradually age, then decline. In China the sharp decline in the death-rate has not been balanced by any marked decline in the birth-rate so that each year has brought an increasing surplus of births over deaths. In these conditions, China is entering on a period of very rapid population growth; today, and in the next few years, the annual increase in her population may well amount to between *one-quarter and one-third of the total annual increase in mankind's numbers*.

Let us look for a moment at the overall picture for China. Let us remember that the Chinese make up one-quarter of humanity, that they are passing through a period of great social and economic change and that the data we have on such things as birth-rates, death-rates and expectation of life must, of necessity, be very approximate. Birth-rates for the country are said to be 37 per thousand population. Death-rates have dropped to 17 per thousand. The surplus of births over deaths, the rate of increase, is thus 20 per thousand, or 2 per cent per annum. The present-day population of China is, in round figures, 700 million, so that the *annual* increase is some 14 million people. This may be an underestimate; some experts believe it may be as high as 17 million. It is difficult to comprehend these figures; even to say that this *increase* is as big as the *total* population of Yugoslavia or of New Zealand and Australia combined gives only an incomplete impression of its magnitude. Perhaps we can express it in terms that are within our own experience by saying that each day China's population increases by an amount equal to the population of a good-sized English market town such as Hereford; that at present rate the increase each week is about equal to the population of a medium-sized city such as Coventry. At this rate of growth China could well have a population of 1,200 million by the end of the century.

Can the Chinese living-space accommodate this growing multitude of Chinese? Can the economy absorb 10, 15, 20 million more workers each year—or will the future bring a gigantic over-spilling into the thinly peopled lands elsewhere in the Pacific area? There is little to support this latter—and widely-held—belief; rather does it seem that, for the foreseeable future, the provision of factories and farms and homes and services for this expanding population (within China itself) will absorb most of the energies of the Chinese People's Government. To provide an improved level of living for her 700 million people, to expand and intensify her economy to provide for the tens of millions yet unborn, China desperately needs peace.

Agricultural expansion is obviously vitally important if this population is to be absorbed. China is still a dominantly rural country and a great proportion of her population increase will have to find its livelihood on the land; the growing cities, too, must be supplied with food. Parts of rural China are already among the most congested areas on earth, supporting 3,000 to 4,000 people per square mile. But two-thirds of China's people are crowded on to one-seventh of China's surface and vast areas support only a scanty population. An increase in agricultural output might be achieved by expanding cultivation in these marginal areas; to many writers in the past this has seemed the obvious solution to China's population problems. However, cultivation of these marginal areas involves a change in technology, since many of these are essentially dry-farming or pastoral areas, and would call for massive quantities of machinery and of fertilisers. At the present stage of China's development this presents obvious difficulties. The Chinese have, therefore, tackled the problem of providing a rising level of consumption for their expanding population by intensification of agriculture on the existing arable area. Their general policy has been to concentrate fertiliser, machinery, irrigation and above all labour on what they term 'high-yielding tracts' and to meet their food problem by wiping out the conditions which created a condition of almost endemic famine in the old days (the vulnerability of the peasant to flood and drought) and by gradually pushing up crop yields. It seems likely that this policy will continue for the measurable future; in the meantime, the marginal areas such as the North-east and parts of China's Far West represent a land reserve which might be developed for food production should the need ever arise at a later date.

One of the major aims of the Chinese government is to expand and widen the industrial sector of the economy. Without industry China would be a helpless and impoverished giant. China has immense resources of the major industrial raw materials; intensive work by geologists and other scientists is opening up each year new resources. The industrialisation described earlier will greatly increase the carrying capacity of the Chinese living space in the decades ahead. We in Britain found this one solution when we faced a population problem similar in character, if not in magnitude, during the 18th and 19th centuries, and the Chinese may well find part of the solution to *their* problem along the same lines.

Finally, what of the official Chinese reaction to this accelerating growth of population? The general picture is clear. Marxist economists and politicians do not recognise the possibility of overpopulation of the type that has preoccupied the Western world from Malthus onwards. They stress that man is a producer as well as a consumer. They believe that under a planned economy production can be expanded to keep pace with, or exceed, the rate of population growth. The Chinese Census Commissioner summed up this viewpoint by describing the population as 'the most precious of all the categories of capital'. Certainly, many of the achievements of the last fifteen years have been the result of 'turning labour into capital'; as Dumont has said, 'the investment of labour is the most important source of saving for all the underdeveloped countries which have inadequate financial resources'. It is true that since 1953 there seems to have been a growing realisation that the rapid rise in numbers to be provided with land and homes and services makes it harder to raise the level per head at which these things can be provided. Further, the very rapid drop in infantile mortality rates, which have fallen from 200 per thousand to less than one-fifth that figure in some areas, is bringing about a change in family attitudes. It is no longer necessary to produce eight or ten children in the hope that two or three may live to carry on the family name. At the same time, women are moving into all sorts of jobs formerly closed to them.

We will not know the result of these changes until the next census. What is worth stressing is that no significant falling-off in the rate of China's population growth is likely in the near future. The reason is simple: China's population, by comparison with the populations of Western countries, is a very 'young' one: 16 per cent of the total—or over 100 million—are under four years of age; 41 per cent—or 266 million—are under 18. The contingent of parents-to-be, of those who will be starting families in the next decade or two, is thus very large and, even if smaller families become more common, the aggregate number of births will continue at a high level. In these conditions, for many years to come, one out of every four babies born in the world will start life in a Chinese cradle, as a citizen of a state as yet unrecognised by a majority of United Nations members.

CHAPTER 9

Land of the 700 Million

CROWDED VALLEYS and plains, stippled or lined with the dark blue and red of peasants in their working clothes, crowds of small gaily clad children in every city and village—these drive home to the traveller two basic features of the geography of China—the intense crowding of many men on little land, and the young and expanding character of her population. Some 700 million people occupy the Chinese living space; of these, some 600 million are concentrated in that part of China lying south-east of a line running from the Yunnan–Tibet boundary to Harbin in the north-east. Even within this area of 'Agricultural China' there are great inequalities in density. Flying south-west from Peking to Sian one sees an abrupt and dramatic change from the loess plain, misted with the green of autumn-sown wheat and checkered with rectangular vegetable plots and compact villages, to the russet brown hills of Shansi, streaked with massive faces of bare rock and grey ribbons of gravel and flecked with scattered patches of green around the diminutive villages. Similarly in South China there is a violent contrast between the humanised greenery of the valley floors, with their staircases of terraces and clustered villages, and the red bare erosion-ravaged hills and steep tree-tufted limestone crags. There are indeed, few areas in the world where gradients of population density are as steep as in East Asia. Parts of China have been continously occupied by man for some four millennia; over this immense period of time he has adjusted his pattern of land use and of settlement to an environment highly differentiated in terms of relief, of soils and of climate. He has assessed this environment in terms of his culture—that of a farming group practising an intensive garden style of cultivation based on grains and on vegetables—and has selected certain areas and rejected or by-passed others. The areas he has chosen have been those lending themselves to intensive use—the alluvial lowlands, the loessial plateaux and the gentle and easily terraced slopes—and for a hundred generations population has accumulated in these favoured areas. Lacking techniques of upland farming and livestock rearing he has rejected the upland areas (leaving them to minority peoples such as the Mongols) or has used them destructively, as a source of firewood or constructional timber and, where the forest vegetation has been destroyed, he has grubbed up the very grass roots to use as fuel. The contrast between the closely settled meticulously cultivated flatlands and the empty ravaged uplands strikes the traveller again and again (Figure 8); the population map repeats in the finest detail the land-forms map or the soil map. And the steady build-up of population in the lowlands has not greatly changed this picture, for once population pressure reached a critical point it was relieved, not by any overlapping on to the marginal uplands, but by the seeking out and occupation of neighbouring river basins and alluvial lowlands. From the North China cradle area, then, there has been a steady southward expansion of Chinese settlement, an expansion which followed selectively the pockets of 'good earth'. In this expansion the Red Basin of Szechwan and the lowlands of the Middle and Lower Yangtse were occupied, then and farther south, the old lake basins of the south-west, the valleys whose alluvium-covered floors probe deep into the uplands of South China, the pockets and occasional wider spreads of fertile soil which are closely hemmed in between the sea and the mountains along the whole of the south-east coast. . . .

Today, some nine-tenths of China's population live on one-sixth of the area of the country. Densities within this peasant *oecumene* exceed 600 persons per square mile or approximately 1,300 per square mile of cultivated land. These densities become more meaningful if compared with other parts of the globe; thus, in some villages of Yunnan between 500 and 600 people may get their living from an area equal to that of an American farm supporting 5–6 people.

Some 500 million people, three-quarters of China's population, are concentrated into four major regions: the North China

Plain, whose level loess and loess-derived soils support a 'dense mat of people', representing in the aggregate over one-quarter of China's population; the lowlands of the Middle and Lower Yangtse valley, containing one-fifth of China's population and with densities (in the delta region) reaching 1,500 per square mile; the Red Basin of Szechwan, where densities locally exceed 1,700 per square mile; lastly, the scattered lowlands, coast plains and deltas of South China. These high-density areas of today coincide strikingly with what Chinese writers have termed the 'key economic areas' of early Chinese history. This historical continuity between these key areas of the past, where agricultural productivity and ease of transport permitted the accumulation of the grain surplus on which political and military power ultimately rested, and the high-density areas of the mid-twentieth century, underlines the remarkable stability of the major features of China's social geography. Above all, it emphasises the rigid control which, for long periods of Chinese history, a highly developed and specialised agricultural system has exerted on the distribution of population in the country.

As in many other developing countries the pace of urbanisation in China has greatly increased in the last two decades. The Chinese, however, have been more fortunate than most nations in that they have managed to avoid the chaos and social disintegration which have resulted from this drift to the cities elsewhere; this has been because their society is, as we have seen, a planned society and some measure of control over population migration is essential if planning is to succeed.

China's total urban population, according to the 1953 Census, was 77 million or 13·2 per cent of the total; of these, 51 million people were living in 420 cities of over 20,000 inhabitants; the distribution of these is shown in Maps 20 and 21; 102 cities had populations of over 100,000, nine of these were 'millionaire cities', with populations of over 1 million. These 'millionaire cities' were as follows:

Shanghai	6,204,417	Canton	1,598,900
Peking	2,768,149	Wuhan	1,427,300
Tiensin	2,693,831	Harbin	1,163,000
Shenyang	2,299,900	Nanking	1,091,600
Chungking	1,772,500		

These giant cities contained almost one-quarter of the total urban population. At the other extreme, almost one-third of the population classed as 'urban' lived in centres of under 20,000 people; these small market and administrative centres

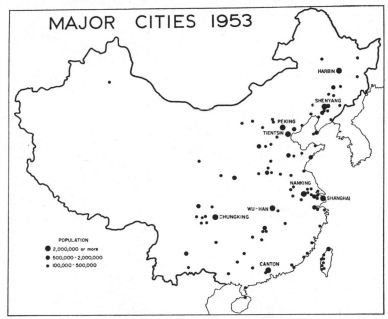

20. Major cities (according to 1953 Census). Major concentrations in east and north-east; urbanisation almost non-existent in Far West.

are, indeed, one of the distinctive elements in the Chinese landscape and some 5,100 of them are listed in the 1953 Census. The proportion of urban dwellers is highest in the industrialised north-east where it is over 30 per cent; the cities of Peking and Tientsin in Hopeh and Shanghai in Kiangsu raise the proportion of urban dwellers for these two provinces to over one-fifth; otherwise, no provinces show percentages of city-dwellers above the national average. Moderate degrees of urbanisation are shown by the south-east coastal provinces of Kwangtung and Fukien (12 per cent) and by the far western regions of Tibet and Sinkiang; urbanisation is of least importance (under five per cent) in the southern interior provinces of Kwangsi and Kweichow.

The urban population seems to have increased by over 140 per cent over the two decades 1938–58, the rate of increase being inversely proportional to the size of city; thus, the group of municipalities which had populations of over one million in 1938 shows a 114 per cent increase in the ensuing twenty years, as compared with a 362 per cent increase for the group of towns with under 50,000 inhabitants. Migration from surrounding rural areas has certainly been a factor contributing to

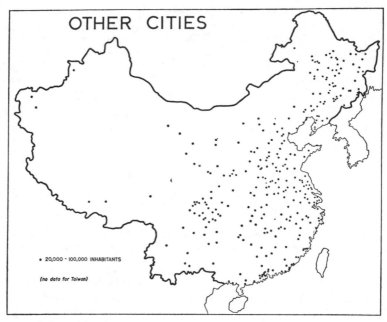

OTHER CITIES

• 20,000 - 100,000 INHABITANTS

(no data for Taiwan)

21. Other cities (according to 1953 Census). Close scatter of smaller cities, mainly administrative centres and market towns. Feeble degree of urbanisation in Far West.

this growth but the 'blind infiltration' of peasants into neighbouring cities has been increasingly controlled by legislation. Natural growth rates in the cities have certainly been high; these rates have exceeded 3 per cent per annum and may have contributed more to the growth of the urban population than has migration. A third way in which the population of some of the major cities has grown has been by territorial expansion of the municipal territory. Several large-scale changes of this type took place in 1958; Peking, for example, quadrupled its area and by the end of 1958 the area under the jurisdiction of Peking municipality was 6,500 square miles. Even more striking has been the extension of the jurisdiction of Tientsin municipality; by the end of 1958 Tientsin's authority covered an area of 7,680 square miles (two-thirds the area of the Netherlands) and a total population of 11·4 million (approximately the population of the Netherlands).

Meanwhile, this expansion of China's urban population finds physical expression in the cultural landscape, in the rapidly extending fringe of factories, dwelling-houses and offices around all the Chinese cities, and in the rebuilding, on spacious multi-storied lines, of cities as far apart as Peking, Lanchow and Kunming. The pace of this re-development is phenomenal; the juxtaposition of the old and the new (Figures 37–48) drives home the progress of the last fifteen years; if the new architecture is often severe or unimaginative these effects are softened by the increasing provision of open spaces and by extensive tree-planting in many of the major cities. And in this re-development each city preserves its distinctive personality: Peking, with its massive grey concrete and granite buildings margining the golden roofs of the old Forbidden City, integrates old and new China; the spacious tree-lined avenues which are replacing the old *hutungs* express the spirit of the new régime; Kunming and Nanning are unfolding in similar fashion, but with a warmth and colour in their architecture and their flowering trees which are unmistakably southern. . . . The list could be extended, but everywhere the picture is the same—a diversity of personalities, in which the best of Traditional China and the aspirations of New China are interwoven.

CHAPTER 10

The Development of China's Intellectual Resources

SINCE 1949 the Chinese have been engaged in a careful and systematic reappraisal of their country's resource endowment; changes in social and economic organisation, in the pattern of industry or of transport are inspired by one major theme—to integrate new resource sectors into the country's economy and to achieve full utilisation of those resources whose existence has long been known but which, for a variety of reasons, have never been fully utilised. China's population falls in this latter category; underemployment or unemployment emphasised that even *quantitatively* full utilisation of this resource was far from being achieved, while widespread illiteracy and the lack of any opportunity for technical training meant that even those who *were* employed could contribute only at the simplest and most rudimentary level. 'Overpopulation' in old China was due very largely to this lack of education and technical skills, for this lack effectively prevented the development of a diversified economy, and condemned the great majority of the population to a poverty-stricken rural existence. Against this background, the geographical importance of the present Government's educational policy becomes apparent; the drive against illiteracy, the rapid expansion of educational facilities at all levels, and the heavy emphasis on technical training—all these will make possible full utilisation of China's biggest resource—the industry and competence of her 700 million citizens. This development is no less important than the uncovering of new physical resources; indeed, the effective realisation of China's ambitious plans of economic development may hinge more on the success of her educational drive than on any other single factor.

In 1949 over four-fifths of China's population was illiterate, education was a privilege enjoyed by a favoured few, skilled technicians were rare and highly trained scientists and research workers rarer still. In these conditions the tasks facing the People's Government in the education field were clear: to teach the masses to read and to write; to expand the school system to bring in as many children as rapidly as possible; to train an increasing number of skilled and semi-skilled workers and, by the development of advanced education and research institutes, to expand greatly the country's resources of scientific man-power. Only if these tasks were achieved could the objectives which the Chinese economic planners had formulated be attained; in the words of an American report 'they had to insure the present and future needs of the country with the skilled man-power needed to achieve their objectives'.

The drive against illiteracy aimed at eliminating illiteracy by 1963-4; by 1958 some 40 million people were attending anti-illiteracy classes and another 31 million were attending spare-time secondary or primary classes. It is true that the standard for minimal adult literacy is set relatively low—for peasants it means 1,500 characters and for urban workers 2,000 characters —and with this level of competence it will be possible to read only the most simple type of text. Nevertheless, 'to have raised (by 1957) some 22 million illiterates even to this minimum standard of literacy through spare-time study must be considered a major accomplishment'. The extension of literacy is being facilitated by two important linguistic reforms—the introduction of simplified versions of Chinese characters and the introduction of a more or less phonetic romanised script. This romanisation comes up against the difficulty posed by the diversity of Chinese dialects and can be successful only if one dialect (e.g. the Peking dialect) is taught throughout the country; it should moreover be emphasised that the aim of this reform is not to replace the Chinese characters with the phonetic alphabet but merely to speed up the learning process. This drive against illiteracy was especially important in the minority regions where new non-Chinese scripts have been devised for groups who formerly had no written language.

The progress in the field of formal education is indicated by the fact that, in less than a decade, enrolment in primary schools increased by 60 millions and in institutes of higher education by 500 per cent. This rapid increase has inevitably involved some sacrifices of quality—in 1956, for example, two-fifths of the primary school teachers had not completed their junior secondary education—and this is recognised by the Chinese who regard it as a transitional phenomenon. Expenditure on education has represented in recent years one-tenth of the expenditure in the State Budget. The 'Great Leap Forward' in 1958 brought a rapid increase in numbers attending educational institutions of all types; it also saw the initiation of a policy of integrating education and productive work. Universities, secondary schools and primary schools set up small factories in which the pupils received technical training and which helped, if only on a small scale, to boost output figures and to defray the cost of the pupils' training. At the same time, there was a rapid increase in the number of schools operated by factories, by communes, by street committees and similar bodies. Many were of a spare-time variety, with little equipment and staffed by teachers with minimal levels of training. These schools were designed to be self-supporting and to supplement those operated by the State and their development has enabled the State to pass on to the masses part of the financial burden imposed by the rapid growth in student numbers. The educational policy, like the economic policy, is one of 'walking on two legs'.

Among the various sectors of the educational system, primary school enrolments have gone up from 24 million in 1949 to 90 million in 1959–60; secondary general schools have increased their enrolment from one million in 1949 to 8·5 million in 1958–9; secondary specialised schools (teacher-training and vocational schools) had 1·4 million students in 1958–9. The numbers enrolled in institutes of higher education rose from 117,000 in 1949 to 810,000 in 1959–60; of these, almost one-quarter were spare-time students.

The ultimate placing of graduates is determined by the State Economic Commission in the light of the country's needs; thus, in 1956, 24 per cent of the graduates were to be sent abroad or to advanced research institutes, 25 per cent went to departments and agencies of the Ministry of Heavy Industry and 34 per cent to the service of the provinces, the Autonomous Regions or the municipalities.

There is likely to be a continuing shortage of highly skilled technical personnel for some time to come and the increasing numbers of technicians being trained will make a considerable contribution to China's present economy and will play a critical role in determining its future rate of growth. No less significant are the achievements at the other end of the educational scale—the wiping out of illiteracy among the masses and the foundations which have been laid for a system of universal education. Inevitably, the programme of educational development has had to be a 'crash programme' in which quality has had to be sacrificed to quantity; in such conditions any comparison between present-day levels of educational attainment in China and those of a country such as New Zealand is meaningless and irrelevant. But, once the foundations have been well and truly laid, rising levels of general education and of technical competence will progressively reduce the advantages at present enjoyed by the West and will introduce a new dynamism into the social geography of the Chinese Peoples Republic. The tremendous scientific and educational achievements of the Soviet Union, and the implications of these, are only now beginning to be realised by the West; the emergence of China as an economic and a scientific giant of the same order will have even more momentous consequences for the world in which those of you who are still at school will be living.

CHAPTER 11

A Personal Summing-up

I MUST DRAW to a close. I could speak of other things—of the gentleness and the earnest dedication of the interpreter who accompanied me on my last visit to China, of the enthusiasm and the modesty with which commune members showed me the factories and dykes and irrigation systems and schools they had built with their own hands. I could talk of the many kindnesses received and the friendships which somehow surmounted the barriers of language. I could try to capture for you in words something of the colour and scents and sounds of China; the blue and gold roofs of Peking's temples, the red flames of peasant blast furnaces in the grey light of dawn, the deep blue sky and yellow dust of Lanchow, the warm wheaten colour, flushed with red, of a girl's cheek in Sian, the orange earth and blue cloud-marbled lake of Kunming, the scarlet of drying peppers and the rustling dark brown of the millet. . . . The scent of cooking oil and dung and of sun on the hot earth. . . . The mellow tinkling of donkey bells, the agonising squeak of barrows, the high thin note of the Chinese flute and the endless whispering of bamboo fronds and the shrilling of cicadas. Even the black-and-white illustrations to this booklet may help you to capture something of this quality of the Chinese earth, of the way of life of the Chinese people.

My impressions? A country still poor by Western standards but with a rising level of living. Crowded counters in the shops and a surprising range of goods to buy. Children healthy, well cared for, and happy. A people working with an energy and a dedication unmatched elsewhere—with the visible results of their efforts in the shape of new schools and flats and factories to spur them on. . . . A people dedicated to peace, engaged in

82

a vast war against poverty, in a campaign to reshape their environment that will take years to complete. All the long-range development plans I saw, all the massive changes I have described, rest on the fundamental assumption of peace; without peace they would be little more than 'A tale told by an idiot, signifying nothing. . . .'

This accelerating transformation of China discussed in the foregoing pages is of vital importance to the world—and it has a lesson for us as geographers. It illustrates how the release of human energies and enthusiasm through a social and political revolution makes possible the creation of an entirely new relationship between man and his environment. It illustrates how, in the shaping of this new environment, new needs and new opportunities bring into being new forms of social organisation (such as the commune). And if, as seems likely, the Chinese experiment succeeds, this success will have a major impact on the uncommitted countries of South and East Asia. The creation within the framework of a Communist society of a new world of plenty would be taken as evidence of the superiority of that society by the small and struggling nations of China's southern fringes. And at that moment, a new world power balance would be struck.

APPENDIX 1

Some Chinese Syllables in Place Names

Ho	*river*	Pei	*embankment, shore, north*
Hu	*lake*	Sha	*sand, gravel, sandbank*
Kiang	*river*	Shan	*hill, mountain, hilly island*
King	*capital city*	Si (Hsi)	*west*
Kwang	*broad*	T'ang	*embankment, pool*
Ling	*mountain range*	Tung	*east*
Men	*door, gate, pass*	Wan	*bay*
Nan	*south*	Yun	*clouds*

Thus Peking is 'the northern capital', Nanking (the former capital) is 'the southern capital' Si Kiang is 'the west river'; Yunnan is the province 'south of the clouds' (referring to the heavy cloud cover typical of the Red Basin to the north).

APPENDIX 2

Sample Details of Selected Communes

The communes selected are chosen from some two dozen visited by the writer in the course of field-work in China in 1958 and 1964. The details for the first four communes relate to 1958; those for the last two to 1964.

1

Commune near Peking: Population 22,500 households of which 9,000 were peasant households, grouped in 129 villages. Area 10,000 acres. Formed by merging of eight co-operatives. Emphasis on vegetable growing, including glasshouse cultivation. 14 Tractors.

2

Commune near Lanchow: Population 3,000 households. Emphasis on irrigated production of vegetables and fruit, with some wheat and maize. Stock included 4,000 pigs, 3,000 sheep, 110 milk cows (an innovation), 20,000 poultry and 70 hives of bees, 5 tractors, 1 lorry. Commune ran 12 primary schools, 1 middle school and a veterinary school.

3

Commune near Chengtu: Population 14,500 households. 18,000 acres under crops, mainly rice, with wheat, vegetables, tobacco, potatoes and hemp. Livestock included 35,000 pigs, 2,000 oxen. Commune possessed 5 tractors, and ran a wide range of industries such as woodworking and alkali manufacture. It ran 286 dining halls, 282 nurseries, 119 kindergartens and 39 primary schools.

4

Minority (Yi) Commune, near Kunming: Population 4,800 families. 9,000 acres of land, one-third irrigated lowland, two-thirds hill land Stock: 4,000 buffalo and oxen, 6,300 sheep, 10,500 pigs. The commune ran native-style blast furnaces, turning out some 20 tons of pig iron weekly; 20 brick kilns; limekilns; and wood-working industries including simple agricultural machinery.

5

Commune in Pearl River delta, west of Canton: Population 6,800 families (24,500 people). Area 4,000 acres, of which one-half was under irrigated rice, one-quarter devoted to fishponds and one-quarter to dry-land crops. It was broken up for operational purposes into 15 production brigades, grouping 137 production teams. 3 lorries, 6 tractors (two-fifths of area were cultivated by machinery). Owned 620 water buffalo and produced 5,000 pigs yearly; each family had some 20–30 poultry and a small plot of land as its private property. The commune's industries—quarrying, brickmaking, building, machine workshops and the like—employed 500 people. It ran 19 primary schools and 15 nurseries for the children of its members. Formerly at the mercy of floods it had constructed 36 pumping stations (aggregate horse-power 2,400) to provide drainage and irrigation.

6

Commune on hilly margin of Pearl River lowland, north of Canton: Population 11,000 families (51,000 people). Area 50,000 acres, of which seven-tenths were rolling and uncultivated hill country; four-fifths of the lowland area was under rice, the rest under fruit, groundnuts and miscellaneous crops or fish ponds. Was formed by merging of 56 cooperatives and organised for operation purposes into 24 production brigades grouping 365 production teams. Commune had 6 lorries and 25 tractors which cultivated 45 per cent of the rice area. Had a total of 40,000 pigs. Its industries employed 582 people and included pottery, brick and tile making, woodworking, manufacture of simple machine tools, mining of coal and lime-burning. The commune ran a total of 55 primary schools, one middle school, 8 clinics and a small hospital. Formerly the commune suffered greatly from drought but since 1958 commune members have constructed a major irrigation canal 15 miles long and reservoirs with an aggregate water-storage capacity of 45 million cubic metres. 92 electric pumps were installed and today 95 per cent of the cropland is irrigated.

APPENDIX 3

Some Background Books

(Paperbacks are indicated by an asterisk)

GENERAL WORKS

Adler, S., *The Chinese Economy*, Routledge and Kegan Paul, London, 1957.

Belden, J., *China Shakes the World*, Gollancz, London, 1952.

Writers for 'China Reconstructs', *China in Transition*, Peking, 1957.

Crook, D. and I., *Revolution in a Chinese Village*, Routledge and Kegan Paul, London, 1959.

*Fitzgerald, C. P., *The Chinese View of their Place in the World*, O.U.P., London, 1964.

Fitzgerald, C. P., *Floodtide in China*, Cresset, London, 1958.

Greene, F., *The Wall has Two Sides*, Cape, London, 1962.

Ho, Ping-ti, *Studies on the Population of China*, Cambridge, Mass., 1959.

*Huberman, L. and Sweezy, P., *China Shakes the World Again*, Monthly Review Press, New York, 1959.

*Hudson, G. F., *Europe and China*, Beacon, Boston, 1961.

Hughes, T. J. and Luard, D. E. T., *Economic Development of Communist China*, O.U.P., London, 1959.

*Lethbridge, H. J., *The Peasant and the Communes*, Dragonfly Books, Hong Kong, 1963.

*Kuo, Ping-chia, *China*, O.U.P., London, 1963.

*Kuo, Ping-chia, *China: New Age and New Outlook*, Penguin, Harmondsworth, 1960.

Mende, T., *China and her Shadow*, Thames and Hudson, London, 1961.

Myrdal, Jan, *Report from a Chinese Village*, Heinemann, London, 1965.

Orr, Lord Boyd, and Townsend, P., *What's Happening in China?* Macdonald, London, 1959.

Purcell, V., *China*, Benn, London, 1962.

Roy, C., *Into China*, Sidgwick and Jackson, London, 1955.

*Snow, E., *Red Star over China*, Grove Press, New York, 1961.

Snow, E., *The Other Side of the River*, Gollancz, London, 1963.
del Vayo, J. A., *China Triumphs*, Monthly Review Press, New York, 1965.
*Wylie, M., *The Children of China*, Dragonfly Books, Hong Kong, 1962.

PERSONAL MEMOIRS

Bodde, D., *Peking Diary*, Cape, London, 1951.
Hua, Su, *Ancient Melodies*, Hogarth Press, London, 1953.
Payne, R., *Chungking Diary*, Heinemann, London, 1945.
Suyin, Han, *Destination Chungking*, Cape, London, 1953.
Thai, Vinh, *Ancestral Voices*, Collins, London, 1956.

ILLUSTRATED WORKS

Cartier-Bresson, H., *China*, Bantam, New York, 1964.
Cartier-Bresson, H., *China in Transition*, Thames and Hudson, London, 1956.
Forman, W. and B., *The Face of Ancient China* (contains some super-lative photos of *modern* China), Spring Books, London, 1960.
Hajek, L., Hoffmeister, A., and Rychterova, Eva, *Contemporary Chinese Painting*, Spring Books, London, 1961.
Glimpses of China, Peking, 1958.
People's Communes in Pictures, Peking, 1960.

POETRY

It has been said: 'If you wish to understand China at all, you must read her poetry.' The anthologies listed below capture something of the quality of Chinese life through the ages and of the dreams and aspirations of her people.
*Bynner, W., *The Jade Mountain*, Doubleday, New York, 1964.
*Davis, A. R. (Editor), *The Penguin Book of Chinese Verse*, Harmondsworth, 1962.
*Hsu, Kai-yu (Editor and Trans.) *Twentieth-Century Chinese Poetry*, Doubleday, New York, 1963.
Kuo Mo-jo and Chou Yang, *Songs of the Red Flag*, Peking, 1961.
*Payne, R., *The White Pony*, Mentor, Books New York, 1960.

NOVELS

Buck, Pearl, *The Good Earth*
Buck, Pearl, *The Mother* } numerous editions.
Hersey, J., *A Single Pebble*, Hamilton, London, 1956.
King, E., *Children of the Black-haired People*, M. Joseph, London, 1956.

SOME BACKGROUND BOOKS

PERIODICALS

China Quarterly, London.
China Pictorial, Peking.
China Reconstructs, Peking.
Eastern Horizon, Hong Kong.
Pacific Viewpoint, Wellington.

Index

(Map and plate references are marked by single and double asterisks respectively)